SIMPLE TREASURES
IN
- BULGARIA -

BULGARIA'S HIDDEN TREASURES DISCOVERED BY AN EXPATRIATE WHO LIVES AND WORKS THERE

by

Martin Miller-Yianni

Publisher: **Martin Miller-Yianni**
Yambol
Bulgaria

First Published (paperback) 2008
Second Edition (hardback) 2010

ISBN 978-1-5173-6316-1

All rights reserved. No part of this publication may be reproduced, stored in a retrieval system, or transmitted, in any form or by any means, without the prior permission in writing of the publisher, nor be otherwise circulated in any form of binding or cover other than that in which it is published and without a similar condition including this condition being imposed on the subsequent purchaser.

Copyright © Martin Miller-Yianni

A CIP catalogue record for this book is available from the British Library

About the Author

Martin Miller-Yianni was born in Erith, England in 1958 into a working class family. The former primary school teacher is now firmly rooted in the southeastern Bulgarian town of Yambol. Since he first arrived in Bulgaria in 2005 he has been totally immersed in Bulgarian life and culture, which continues to inspire him to write. Having worked in Bulgaria as a writer and researcher for a leading Bulgarian information website, his knowledge, understanding and experience of Bulgarian ways has been well grounded. Now returning to writing freelance, he continues his life with Bulgarians deep within their family and community based culture; a new and better life, which he is now very much part of.

Foreword

Simple Treasures in Bulgaria was written to give a little taste of Bulgaria. An insight into how life is lived by Bulgarians is shown throughout this book. A great deal of pleasure was derived from looking at the fascinating ways things are thought through and done by Bulgarians.

Bulgaria's unique way of life will now become somewhat diluted with the country's inclusion in the European Union. Conforming to rules and regulations, it will soon become uniform with the rest of Western Europe. Bulgaria will have to fall in line and give up much of its charm, character and individualism. Therefore the simple cultural treasures found and recorded in this book I hope will be a contribution to the archives of how Bulgaria was.

I am extremely fortunate that Galia my Bulgarian partner is here by my side. Without her and her family alongside supporting (and feeding me) the material might well have been very different looking in from the outside rather than from within. I therefore willingly dedicate this book to them.

Notes:

- All chapters written using 'I' as the first person were written before meeting Galia. This is just to account for any inconsistencies while reading between 'I' and 'we'

- GSM means mobile phone.

- Some of the characters names have been changed for good reason to protect their true identities.

Leaving the UK wasn't a hard decision to make for the author. There aren't many things he misses, but he does miss his daughter and three sons, Hannah, Peter, Simeon and Nathan respectively. He remains very proud all of their achievements in their lives with his absence.

--- List of Treasures ---

Page

About the Author..3
Forward..4
Contents..6

1. Living Off the Bulgarian Land 8
2. Shopska Salad Recipe 14
3. The Healing Stones Of Skalitsa 16
4. Sirni Zagovezni 18
5. Bloody Starlings! 20
6. Skalitsa Man from Eden to Heaven 23
7. The Village Hairdresser - Beware! 27
8. Indoor Cricket 29
9. Skalitsa Banitsa Recipe 31
10. Mice in Bulgaria 33
11. Skalitsa Maestros 36
12. In Bulgaria? You'll Do This Soon! 42
13. Bulgarian Weather Talk 44
14. Bulgarian Village Life — A Glimpse 46
15. Litterbugs 54
16. The Bulgarian Door 56
17. Tarator Recipe 61
18. Healing Stones – More Evidence! 62
19. Bulging Bulgarian Buses 64
20. Alternative Medicine in Bulgaria 68
21. A Sorry Dog Tale in Bulgaria 72
22. Rakia Experiences 74
23. A Bargain Weekend Holiday 77
24. Shkembe Chorba – An Early Intro. 80
25. Bulgarian Tundzha Fish...83
26. Bulgarian Tundzha Fishing 85
27. Bulgarian Bikes and Roma Riders 87
28. Yambol Fashion 89
29. Bulgarian Crime — The Attraction 90
30. Schools or Fashion Houses? 93
31. Bulgarian Police — How it is Here 95
32. New Bulgarian Cowboys 101
33. Cobblestone Yambol 103
34. Bulgarian Birthday Party 105
35. Ugly Bulgarian Baby - Not! 108

36.	Ground and Cooled Coffee	110
37.	Bad Brits in Bulgaria	113
38.	Well-Behaved Bees	115
39.	Bulgarian Trees	117
40.	Gardens and Maintenance	119
41.	'New' Fire Engines in Yambol?	121
42.	A Lottery in Bulgaria	124
43.	Small Talk	126
44.	Sofia Without Apples	128
45.	Sofia City, Saturday Night	130
46.	Ladas and Rats	135
47.	Where is Maria?	137
48.	Food from Baba Mama	140
49.	Lada Tyres	143
50.	Working Bulgarians	145
51.	A Bulgarian MOT	147
52.	Another Bulgarian Door	150
53.	A Bulgarian Van	152
54.	Two Bulgarian Restaurants	154
55.	A Memorable Bulgarian Meal	162
56.	Malomir Liqueur Recipe	165
57.	A Funny Thing About Gabrovo	167
58.	The Fat of the Land	169
59.	Coriander	173
60.	Bulgarians Make, Don't Buy!	175
61.	Box of Bulgarian Chocolates	177
62.	Gardening in Bulgarian Graves	180
63.	Bulgarian Tattoos Forever	185
64.	Gergyovden	189
65.	Monster Banks in Yambol	193
66.	Outside Toilets Preferred	196
67.	Shoppe Style Cheese Recipe	198
68.	An Evening With Rano	199
69.	Handbags for Bulgarian Men	204
70.	Snake Talk	206
71.	Sarmi Recipe	210
72.	Another Taste of Heaven	212

SIMPLE TREASURE - 1

- Living Off the Bulgarian Land -

Food here in Bulgaria is something else — every day a new experience is to be had in Bulgarian cuisine. I must say that it helps tremendously that my partner is Bulgarian and cooks like an angel, but that aside, the Bulgarian friends and neighbours still tickle my taste buds at every opportunity with their own cooking. Since coming here there hasn't really been any moment where a pang for supermarket branded food has called out. No Twiglets, Mars Bars, baked beans or even sherbet fountains with the liquorice sticking out felt needed or wanted. In fact nowadays the only thing I can remember about these foods is the horrible aftertaste! People accustomed to eating natural Bulgarian food for long enough here will know exactly what I mean.

Every few weeks someone asks, 'I'm coming over, what would you like me to bring for you?' It is very difficult to think of anything, even after really thinking hard. So these kind people usually bring over some English teabags, Cadbury's Crème Eggs or a bottle of whisky; many thanks guys, and I mean this most sincerely, but these are then actually used for English guests that come round, so very useful anyway. This is not being ungracious, but just speaking truthfully about how things are now.

Here in Bulgaria, most produce comes straight out of the village homes, most of which are not just homes but smallholdings. Food comes from a variety of sources, mainly grown from the rich, dark, fertile land. This produce also feeds chickens, cows and calves, goats and sheep, ducks and geese, rabbits and peafowl, to name a few. Back in the village of Skalitsa where I live, there is no need for supermarket shopping. Occasionally food is bought from the supermarket, more out of habit if I happen to be in town, but usually from my local village shop that provides everything I need: bread and flour (both made and milled in my village), sunflower oil (locally produced), salt and sugar. Local honey is more often used for sweetening than sugar. Filo pastry is also sometimes bought for the homemade banitsas — the recipe for the unique Skalitsa banitsa is further on in the book, but there are other pastry variations of the banitsa throughout Bulgaria. Last but not least, beer: making your own beer is not entertained, as it would never touch the quality that the Belgian brewery owners achieve here. You just can't improve on perfect beer.

    I can't say there is much else needed. As much wine, rakia and liqueur as I could ever wish for is all locally produced in the village or on my own farm. Sunflower seeds are gathered from the field adjoining my land, and as long as it is for personal consumption there is no problem with this; in fact, the mice in the field eat more than any villager. They are dried (some salted) and stored in airtight, recycled plastic food boxes. Chickpeas are grown and stored in the same way; sweetcorn is grown or again taken in from fields and dried (but not used for animal feed — that wouldn't be right if taken from the co-operative fields) and fried in oil to make popcorn: another treat from the garden, flavoured either with honey or salt before popping. So there's your little variety of snacks to accompany your drinks.

    All the cheeses and yoghurts are homemade and all from natural ingredients. Walnuts are gathered and keep for up to a year for use in cooking. Walnuts baked in honey are another Bulgarian food legend, and also used as another accompaniment to drinks. Almonds are harvested, with shells you can remove without nutcrackers; ever tried that with a supermarket almond? Fresh figs are preserved in syrup. There are melons galore, both the honeydew and water type; the latter makes a marvellous jam to be eaten all year round. Strawberry jam used for cakes and for milkshakes is a summer taste second to none. Apples, pears and sliva can all be stored in boxes or bottled in syrup and kept for up to six months. My last apple, eaten in April this year, was almost as good as it would have been picked in October the year before. And it was sweet and tasted like an apple!

On occasion non-Bulgarian guests visit and sometimes turn their nose up at some of the food offered because it's not like the food they're used to buying in shops. You may well be surprised at how many say that! This is the only other reason that supermarkets are frequented, to cater for the need of these occasions. No offence is taken at this point; it's not their fault, it's the system they have grown to rely on. All the produce that is not in season has been either frozen or bottled, and supplies take us through the winter and spring. This is not a chore — the garlic and onions are plaited and the tomatoes, peppers, potatoes and pumpkins boiled for bottling on the outside wood-burning contraption. Everything is done slowly and very systematically. When it comes to doing anything like this in village life there is never any panic or rush with the long day ahead. Why do we, on the other hand, still try and hurry things to get them done as quickly as possible all the time?

With all this food to hand, including most meats and a range of poultry and dairy products, you can make anything you want from the ingredients. Even beef can be grown, bought or bartered for in the village. Everything and more is grown here compared to the UK. So what's the problem there? Nothing, it would seem — the problem in the UK for many is the culture of buying convenience food rather than growing your own. How many have a garden where produce can be grown? Most people. The climate here helps a lot, but what makes it work here is the way of life and the homegrown food culture, which left the UK some 40-50 years ago. You come to Bulgaria and take a big step back in time. I'm always amazed at how the simplest ingredients can turn out to be another memorable meal. Just a sliced young marrow fresh from the garden, dipped in flour and fried until brown, then served hot topped with homemade yoghurt. It was that simple, but the result was something very special. Everyday another taste or recipe is laid out and enjoyed; it really is going back to basic ingredients and enjoying them for what they are. How often is this forgotten, bowing to commercially processed foods made for you from a point of ease and laziness? For convenience, the process squeezes out the taste of natural foods with chemically enhanced products as the replacement, and this becomes the 'taste of the norm' for the weekly consumers. Food regulations introduced is understandable to protect health, but it has gone to extremes and the very chemicals that are meant to protect such as preservatives, flavour enhancements and added colouring, etc. is just as bad if not worse for our long term health.

It is quite strange that most village folk don't have a choice of shopping for food over growing their own food; they simply can't afford it. If they could afford to and had a choice the convenience foods are there, waiting in the wings, ready to pounce for profits, which is the name of the game. The new generation of Bulgarians is making its way to becoming part of the American and Euro fast food brigade. The traditional horticultural activities carried out in villages throughout Bulgaria may end up being restricted to commercial dimensions, as they were in the UK so many years ago. I am grateful and privileged to have the opportunity to experience Bulgaria as it is now.

There's one old wives tale that I continually hear, concerning eggs. The chickens I keep are totally free range, with access to all-natural food in the big yard and greenery from the waste organic vegetation, and a supplement of natural wheat to call them home in the evening. Nothing could be more free range than these chickens. So when someone says, 'Oh, I tried some free range eggs and the colour of the yolk was so deep in colour, it was orange,' I'm a little dubious. Do you have a picture of this apparently fresh free-range egg now revealing its sensuous lush orange yolk, just waiting to melt in the mouth after being lightly fried in a little oil and laid on a bed of the softest white buttered bread you could imagine? Looks good? Tastes good? Doubt it! This is not true; the colour of free-range eggs is usually just plain yellow at best. Battery and commercial egg producers (other than the chickens themselves, of course) use colour additives in the feed to produce a more deeply-coloured yolk, which is what the consumer wants and gets — supply and demand. So the chicken may be described as free-range but what are they given to eat? Market research has found that the yellow yolk doesn't sell as well as the darker orange-tinted colour.

Next time you go to a town supermarket and buy eggs, even so-called free-range ones, see how orange the yolk is; you know why now.

I am still a lifetime away from getting my produce up to the standard of my Bulgarian neighbours: the learning goes on all the time. It is clear that the attitude to food in the UK is that convenience food rules. This is not from the point of choice, many just don't get the choice with their hectic work related lifestyle and a bygone age of daily family table meals. Even if home cooking does happen, ingredients that are used are sourced from supermarkets and also grown in a rush, furthermore hardly ever locally produced and only remains fresh from preservative processes. The difference here in Bulgaria is the food is local, fresh. Along with the culture, the climate, the slow pace of life that been inbred over many generations, you will find that the food grows faster than the pace of life.

SIMPLE TREASURE - 2

- Shopska Salad Recipe -

Shopska salads are unique to Bulgaria; with wonderful complementary ingredients, they make the perfect salad for every occasion.

Ingredients:

400 g red tomatoes
1-2 fresh cucumbers (about 200 g)
1 small hot pepper
150 g white cheese (sirene)
2 medium onions
4 medium green peppers
a few olives
bunch of parsley
sunflower oil
red wine vinegar
salt

Preparation: Peel and chop the onions finely. Clean and remove the stems and the seeds of the green peppers (they can be used with or without the skins) then slice into small rectangles. Chop the hot pepper and cucumber the same way and mix everything together in a big serving bowl. Add salt and mix again. Form a mountain of salad in the bowl or share out onto individual plates or small bowls. Grate or finely chop the sirene over the salad until it resembles a snow-capped mountain, then garnish the peak with a single olive and a few parsley leaves. Add sunflower oil, vinegar and salt to your own taste before mixing and tucking in.

This recipe has a versatility that is second to none. It can be served up on any occasion, at the beginning or at the end of a meal, or even just on its own. If you're serving Bulgarian guests, it's always a good idea to accompany it with a traditional rakia and ayran (a refreshing yoghurt drink) alongside.

SIMPLE TREASURE – 3

- The Healing Stones Of Skalitsa -

Healing stones in my village of Skalitsa have now have affected me, and the claims made for them no longer seem to be wild rumour. Getting older is something that we all have to live with, and aches and pains come with age. A bit of rheumatism had been playing hell with my shoulder for a month, and I had to have painkilling injections to ease it. Now, on the outskirts of Skalitsa there is an area where stones lie on the side of a hill. One of the reasons for choosing this village as a place to live was due to these rocks, said to have healing properties. I had been told that a few years ago a renowned professor from Sofia came to the site and concluded that the rocks are indeed at some magnetic crossing point, and that there are only two places in the world where this phenomenon occurs. There has been a thesis written up on it, and I am in the process of trying to find it.

But I digress; it was a sunny Sunday in January, and both Galia and I — Galia having also had a painful night with her shoulder — decided to take a walk to the healing stones to try the remedy. It was quite a sceptical couple that walked to the site; the stones aren't far from our farm, and our thoughts were on the walk doing us more good than lying on a pile of rocks in the Bulgarian midwinter. It wasn't as bad as we first thought it would be; it was a very clear-skied afternoon, and we spent about an hour lying on a big rock that had been warmed up by the midday sun. There didn't seem to be anything strange happening when we lay there, but amazingly all our aches and pains disappeared! Now whether this was solely down to lying on warm rocks or the healing qualities of the magnetic, fields, we felt a little less sceptical. The following day both of us were still pain free, even on a coldish morning. We intend to revisit next weekend weather permitting. That is assuming that our pains have returned! Right now we are more convinced than before that these stones have healing qualities, and many locals swear by visiting them if they are in pain. One thing is for sure, it is more effective than any other medication that we had taken for the relief of chronic pain! Six months later and still no return of the pain that plagued me for years. Surely this can't just be a coincidence? Why don't more people visit? Why doesn't a wider public know about them? Well, more do now.

SIMPLE TREASURE - 4

- Sirni Zagovezni -

One of the most popular festivals in Bulgaria is Sirni Zagovezni, meaning 'Shrove Sunday' or 'The Great Lent'. This falls each year on a Sunday some seven weeks before Easter. I have experienced two seasons of these now; it is a time for celebrating the beginning of spring and a period of fasting, in fact the longest fasting period of the year in the Orthodox tradition. This means abstaining from meat, dairy products (fish once a week is allowed), no traditional dancing and no marriages to take place until Easter. This fasting does still go on, but the food here is too good and too tempting for me to even consider joining this part of the ritual. Many villages and towns have the tradition of building large bonfires, and Skalitsa is no exception. There is either the usual communal bonfire or individual groups made by neighbours on their own. The fires are built on higher land in the belief that this will prevent hailstorms striking the areas that they light. I live right up on the high ground of the village, so just outside my house is a good place for this. The preparations for this festival include hand-carving wooden rockets and laying them out for a week or two until they are tinder dry for the day. This is really tough on the hands and my carving efforts only resulted in three rockets.

Each rocket is fixed to its launching stick, and then lit from the bonfire before blasting off to challenge the other rockets as they soar up to a hundred metres over the neighbouring houses. As each is launched, a name is shouted out and that rocket subsequently dedicated to that person, family, friend or lover! The handmade rockets are collected up by young Bulgarian maidens — whoever collects the most will be deemed to be the fairest in the town or village. The young male pilots of the rockets therefore usually aim their rockets at their favoured maiden's home to make it easier for her to find. This is a tradition where both young and old gather. The bonfire is the place where asked-for forgiveness is given from the young to the old; a time to rid everyone of past quarrels. This is also traditionally a time for the younger members of the community to respect their elders. Jumping over the fire is another part of the ritual, usually performed by the younger members of the community, although many older members have been known to have a go, and some of them did this cold Sunday evening! It is said that the farthest jump would give that young man a wife in the autumn, but all attempts will give good health to the participants in return for their efforts. I had a go, but graciously let others beat me in distance —the reason being quite simply because I didn't want to get married again!

Even when the rockets and jumping have finished and the wine and rakia have been passed round until they're almost gone the festivities don't stop. This, after all, is the last day of feasting and dancing prior to the fasting period, so it's back home for Bulgarian apple-bobbing, wining, dining and dancing until the early hours; for the morning brings about a focus of the body and mind until Easter. Which was just as well, as I didn't fancy anything to eat in the morning....

SIMPLE TREASURE - 5

- Bloody Starlings! -

The weekend arrived, with the crops this year looking very poor indeed due to the intense heat and lack of rain. The overhanging grapes looked as though they had a hangover, each bunch consisting of various sized grapes, unlike last year when they all were bursting with health and urging the owner to crush them. So, a poor harvest, but at least there was going to be some sort of harvest, I thought. Looking under the trellis I saw that many of the grapes, mostly the ripe ones, had fallen to the ground. I fed these to the chickens, thinking that the wind or the little rain we had in my absence this week must have blown or knocked them off. Whilst lying down at lunchtime with the windows all open, as all Bulgarians do here, I heard a commotion outside. Unable to relax, I upped and viewed the cause. As I appeared outside a great clatter of flapping wings took place, and a split second later a flock of starlings flew out of my vines. They are ugly and ungraceful birds as well, which compounded my anger. 'Bloody starlings!' said the cursing voice that frightened them away. Now I have seen these birds in England, but in Bulgaria they seem to be twice the size, with presumably twice the appetite for my grapes. I felt that they were rubbing salt into the wounds of the poor harvest to turn it into a non-harvest.

Thoughts about how to prevent this happening led to the one immediate plan to remedy the problem: make the vines untouchable. I could cover the whole area with netting, but there would be two problems with this: I would have to buy netting on an industrial scale to cover the whole area; and the fact that this was an English way of solving the problem, something that didn't usually work over here. Asking my Bulgarian neighbours for advice was the immediate next step — surely they would have a solution. I should have known that speaking to my Bulgarian friends about this problem would produce the most Bulgarian way of dealing with it. A shrug of the shoulders and advice that was very difficult for me to come to terms with. The answer was, do nothing: there were enough grapes for everyone, including the starlings; when they're full up, they'll fly away! And anyway, the crop wasn't that good, so why am I worrying?

Well, this didn't really make me feel much better. Had they seen numbers in their thousands flying around the land? Were they aware of the wastage that gets left on the ground, knocked off by all the fluttering around? Somehow I knew the answer would be based around letting nature do the business — it is very Bulgarian to do that. It's their very nature and their different way of thinking that is so different to ours. I often wonder how they cannot be beside themselves with the thought of the thieving starlings taking free pickings while they do nothing. The difference could be between getting a little wine and getting no wine, and that's a big difference in my book. The rest of the weekend was spent trying to come to terms with the Bulgarian way of dealing with starlings: simply to do nothing! Even so, a violent clapping of hands with a simultaneous with hollering of 'BLOODY STARLINGS' occurred every time I made a trip into the garden! This would be a drop in the ocean, as I was due to leave the place for five days. Might as well let them get on with it. Why do I bother while I am there? To a Bulgarian it is regarded as wasted energy and anger that shouldn't be there. It is so hard to think like a Bulgarian, but they are probably right, and the advice is the best I will get — in Bulgaria, anyway.

SIMPLE TREASURE - 6

- Skalitsa Man from Eden to Heaven -

Things change, and this week another chapter closed in the road where I live in Skalitsa. Another member of the Skalitsa community, my closest neighbour Dino, passed away. He was seventy three and fell asleep in a field of sweetcorn, never to wake. A very peaceful ending for a man who never stopped working all his life but, typically for Bulgaria, always had time to talk to people. His wife departed some ten years ago, and now she is reunited with him again in Heaven's garden, having both spent their lives in the Garden of Eden. His family works his farm now, but on a scaled-down level: whether it carries on as a farm or whether it gets put up for sale and turned into an ex-pat home is up in the air at the moment, but the latter is increasingly the trend in the villages.

Dino helped me no end with learning the ropes of farm life and took me into the community with such warmth and friendliness, and I miss him being here now. Dino was a man of small stature; he had a severe curvature of the spine, which left him permanently stooped, quite common in many older- generation smallholders. I never really found out what the cause of this was, whether it was inherited or from the labours of the land. He was well known to everyone, as are all the people who live in Skalitsa. Dino's relationships with most other folk in the village were a strange affair, but they never ever commented on whether they liked him or not. They didn't have an opinion of him; he was just Dino, and nothing else. Of course everyone talks to everyone else all the time here, and Dino was no exception. Often villagers on their way past his farm would pause to sit on the bench outside his farm, talking —

sometimes for hours — as the sun slowly sank below the Bulgarian skyline.

The produce from Dino's farm made him completely self-sufficient, bar bread, lemonade, gas and electricity. He worked very hard, never having taken a day off in his life, a fact I found out when speaking with him one evening. His farm was large and well-stocked, with every food on his doorstep. He made money out of his livestock, and together with his feeble eighty-pounds-a-month pension made ends meet. Every day in the three seasons free food was gathered for his animals from neighbouring community shared lands. Once a week the accumulation of muck was taken away by his horse and cart to one of the Skalitsa village municipal dumps, namely an allocated field up the road! rakia and wine was made on an industrial scale, using his own distilling system in one of his outbuildings.

I remember him taking me in to see his rakia-making in action; he had ten 120-litre barrels, all full of sliva fermenting away. The fumes could have knocked you out there and then! Many an evening, no matter the season, he would come around with a small bottle of homemade rakia and tomatoes, either fresh or bottled depending on the month, and we'd sit in or out and just talk. He considered my rakia better than his, as by the end of the evening it was always my bottle of home-made rakia that had seen its way to the bottom, while his remained untouched. It took quite a while for me to realise that he was a skilled master at poaching other people's rakia by praising it! That was all part of his make up. I always remember him asking me for 1000 leva for a Lada car, as he said his horse was too old now. This was asked for not as a loan but a gift! He thought that this Englishman was laden with gold after seeing the inside of my house, containing what I thought were very humble personal belongings. Even until the day he passed away he was sure that I had more money than I needed, and he never gave up asking me.

He used to swear a lot, something I could tell solely from the tone of his voice; routinely first thing in the morning and last thing at night, with sporadic bouts in between. The main reason for this was that his sheep and goats never ever did what he wanted them to. Most evenings he was chasing them up the path by my house, trying to get them back into their pen, and I often wondered why in his wisdom he hadn't solved problem this many years ago. I would ask him this very question and he would just shrug his shoulders without answer and then carry on where he left off. Yes, he's Bulgarian all right!

Often, when the flocks of sheep and goats trotted by, wandering towards to their well-trodden home pastures, Dino would have forgotten to shut his big farm gate, and flocks of sheep and goats would stroll into his yard to eat the hard-earned hay reserved for his herd. I used to watch this with amusement from my kitchen window, as I knew at any moment the swearing and cursing would start, and then the waving and beating of his stick to get them away from the free feed and back into the road. I would wonder again, after all the years he has been working here, why did this still happen? I didn't bother to ask, as I knew what the answer would be.... The day before he passed away I was helping him pull up his broken water pump from his well, service it and put it back down. It hadn't been working for six months. This was the least I could do, as it had served me well when I'd had no water during my first few months here in Skalitsa. It now worked perfectly after the long period of non-operation. He was a very happy man at this point; he had his well water back, and of course it hadn't cost him anything to fix it. Any Bulgarian would be happy with this, but being Dino it was even more of a happy event.

He loved having his picture taken. The first time I took his photo I gave him a print; a picture of him sitting on the rubble that had been dug out for my septic tank. I went to his house a few months later, around Christmas time, and in his living room, the only picture in the room, and sitting as the main feature on his side cabinet, was this photograph. This made me feel so humble about things I take for granted. Dino was part and parcel of the character of the street and now he's gone; his cursing and nose for good opportunities to poach rakia will be missed. His companionship will also be sorely missed, but most of all the simple fact that you knew that he was there all the time; it may seem quite a strange thing to say, but that how it feels.

So as another chapter unfolds, the older inhabitants in the villages are gradually fading out of the picture, and there is no one to carry on the farming tradition. Towns and cities send out the call of money to the new generations, and you can hardly blame them for seeking a 'better' life for their families. Opportunities in towns, cities, or other European countries for that matter, are ever increasing, leaving a void to be filled in the villages. These homes are turned into holiday or retirement homes for expatriates in the main; others are bought and left vacant as their prices rise. I felt compelled to write about Dino, and so I have, but this epitaph could have been written for many other older generation Bulgarians in villages throughout the country.

- The Village Hairdresser - Beware! -

In a nearby village there's a notorious hairdresser, and if she's anything to go by she is not a good advert for her trade, as she has a moustache herself. Her name is Kremena; she is now an elderly woman. She's been running the business for nearly forty years, and never had a complaint until recently. Her surgery, sorry, *salon*, has never been decorated in all those years and still has the same chair. It is my opinion that she was the inventor of the punk hairstyle. Whenever I get the chance I go there, but only because she is my friend, and to visit friends in the town. It doesn't matter, as many others have the same style and don't complain, so I don't complain either. The cost was 1.50 leva for a short back and sides, with little bonuses thrown in, as some sides are shorter than others. The other service she offers men is a shave. Now, apart from when I had my appendix out, no-one else has ever shaved me before: this was a first for me, and for a fee of 50 stotinki it was actually cheaper than buying a razor blade. Why doesn't everyone go there for a shave then? I was about to find out. It was a nervous man who sat there at the mercy of this old lady, who bore a cutthroat razor of just the type I had feared. I wear glasses due to short-sightedness, and I can't see much without them on, so I couldn't see what was going on in the cracked old mirror facing me; the shave proceeded with me in the dark, so to speak....

When she had finished, homemade rakia was slapped on my face (ouch!) and I was asked to wait in the chair while we talked. Then a damp cloth was wiped over my face, and after paying I was free to go. As usual it took a lifetime to make my back along the streets — I knew a lot of people in this village, and had to stop to chat to them all en route. The curious thing was they normally ask me where I have been and what I've been up to — today, they knew where I'd been and merely asked me where I was going now. I wasn't quite sure how they knew until I finally got back home to Skalitsa and saw the blood-stained face staring back at me from the mirror. It looked as though I had been halfway through the death of a thousand cuts, but all in the same area. Well, 50 stotinki really was cut price, and that's exactly what I got. No wonder everyone knew where I had been. But don't just take my word for it — my brother went there a few weeks later and came back with an Elvis-style sideburn on one side and the original Blackadder style on the other. His face also looked as though it had been through a mincer; you could have made black pudding with the amount of blood that was seeping out. The only difference between his episode and mine was that he had complained! I still go there for a punk haircut now and then, but never for a shave, even though she considers herself a cut above the rest.

SIMPLE TREASURE - 8

- Indoor Cricket -

Last summer many areas of Bulgaria, and certainly rural homes in the southeast of Bulgaria, were overrun with black field crickets, to the point where the locals are forced to spend money (a rare occurrence in villages) on poison to control the numbers that invaded their homes. Bucketfuls of these creatures swarmed into homes and buildings, a nightmare for those who fear these relatively harmless insects. It started around the beginning of July, sparked off by the very poor season of sunflowers, sweetcorn, and many other crops that should have been in their prime at this time. The poor field crickets found themselves without their normal sources of food, such as seeds, plants or smaller insects. They are known to feed on grasshopper eggs, moth pupae, butterflies and flies, even stealing spiders' meals from their webs. So a lack of their natural diet led the Bulgarian field cricket community to find other sources of food, and inevitably homes and buildings are a rich alternative source for them, where so many other food supplies and insects hang out.

Southeast Bulgaria has the least density in population in comparison to other regions, with vast areas of agricultural land surrounding tiny villages. Along with the poor crop, this creating an unprecedented situation, where literally swarms of Bulgarian field crickets descended on the villages to look for other food sources to survive. Where does this leave the country dweller? Well, the vast majority of these crickets invade Bulgarian households, just to be swept away every few hours. Cats, chickens, other wildfowl and mice regard them as tasty snacks, so the outbuildings are pretty much taken care of. The biggest problem is actually in the living area, where of course in Bulgaria no livestock or pets are allowed. That makes it the humans' problem, and as far as the Bulgarian village dweller is concerned just another chore to deal with as part of the daily routine. This has happened before in poor seasons and is accepted as part and parcel of country living; and the foreigners who moved here for the idyllic Bulgarian lifestyle get a taste of its occasional grim realities.

Due to the nature of Bulgarian construction the typical Bulgarian home can have many access points: the crickets squeeze in through gaps in poorly fitted doors, cracks in window frames, through foundations, attics and light fittings, chimney vents and poorly fitted ceiling coving. Well-renovated homes built to western European standards have much less of a problem: all you really have to do is keep the doors and windows shut. This is not really any hardship if fly screens are part of the renovation — these crickets have become a barometer as to how well your house has been renovated! Other preventative measures can be put in place, but the only really effective one is laying powdered insecticide around the perimeter of the home and sweeping up the remains each morning. I don't like using poison inside the house, so on the odd occasion I see one I suck them up with a rechargeable hand Hoover and give the contents to the chickens in the morning. Fortunately this is a game of limited overs, and the cricket season ends with the first cold night; the numbers decrease leading up to this, and all will eventually die with the first frost. Hopefully the next cricket season will stay firmly on Sky Sport TV. Mind you, some prefer the insects to the actual game!

SIMPLE TREASURE - 9

- Skalitsa Banitsa Recipe -

This is probably the most famous Bulgarian recipe bar shopska salad, and with the pastry now bought in a ready-to-use form from shops it is very simple to make. This particular recipe was given to me by my Bulgarian neighbour called Rosa, she is the local nursery schoolteacher. It is as far as I'm aware only local to my village, Skalitsa, which (in my totally unbiased opinion) gives better results than the original national recipe, hence the name 'Skalitsa Banitsa'.

Ingredients: all the ingredients are readily available in most villages and in every town and city in Bulgaria.

One packet (500 gm) of filo pastry
3 eggs
1 cup plain flour
1 cup yoghurt
1 tablespoon baking powder
sunflower oil
chopped sirene (Bulgarian white cheese)

If you are not in Bulgaria you can use self-raising flour instead of the plain flour and baking powder, and feta or cottage cheese (adding a bit more salt) instead of sirene.

Step-by-step method:

Preheat the oven to 170°C. Put the eggs, flour, baking powder and yoghurt in a bowl, mix well and put to one side. Unwrap the pastry and lay all the sheets on the plastic wrapping on the work surface. Lightly grease a baking tray big enough to take the width of the pastry when rolled up. Trickle oil over the top layer of the pastry, then dribble the mixture randomly over the pastry and sprinkle sirene evenly over the top. Taking two layers of filo pastry at a time, roll and place it on the baking tray (make sure you roll the pastry very loosely). Repeat the process until all the sheets of pastry have been used, and if there's any mixture left over brush the top of the parcels in the tray with it; if there is none left, brush some oil over the top of the banitsas. Place the tray in hot oven and bake for 20 minutes.

These are best eaten hot, or they can be reheated or eaten cold later in the day. I make Skalitsa banitsas without fail every Saturday, and eat them, reheated for a minute or so in a microwave every morning, for breakfast. A good Bulgarian tip: to get the sunflower oil to spread evenly over the pastry, simply pierce a small hole in the top of the plastic bottle cap and use it as a squeezy bottle.

SIMPLE TREASURE - 10

- Mice in Bulgaria -

You will never really get rid of mice in Bulgaria, especially in the country regions. Once one clan of mice have gone other clans will arrive. Whether they stay or not is down to the surroundings and environment; just like house-hunting really. Bulgarians in the main, especially in the villages, live with the mice and look at this as a minor inconvenience. They do try and take sensible steps, with traps and poison, but the odd mouse or two is not deemed a major problem. They accept that mice are a part and parcel of their living space and live, if not quite happily alongside them, contently enough in most cases. Rats are a different story and are looked upon in a very different light. This would require another chapter in another book.

Bulgarian mice are very simple creatures and you have to put yourself into their frame of mind before knowing how to cope with them. Survival is the key element, not only from the point of an individual mouse but also from a mice family perspective. Imagine you're a mouse just out of nappies, on your own with hormones running wild; what do you need? Well let's list a few things for starters: a warm, safe and draught free home; a food supply; a water supply; a family. This short list of basic requirements is not too dissimilar from our own needs. Understanding this gives you a slight edge in the battle to rid your house of mice: changing the environment they would favour. The first step is to ensure that all food in the house is not left out and floors are kept clean and free from crumbs. There is no particular favourite place for mice in houses, as each room has its own attractions. The kitchen or dining room is well known to mice, a source of scraps, or more plentiful supplies from cupboards where food isn't stored in mouse-proof containers. Tupperware and glass containers are the answer: not only are they impervious to mice gnawing through them, as they do with cardboard containers, they help keep the food stocks fresher for longer as well. I invariably use these plastic or glass containers to store food directly after they it is bought — all recycled, of course!

Kitchen drawers are another favourite haunt where mice can find resources they need for their home. Drawers or cupboards full of tea towels and aprons are regarded by mice as luxury bedding, or a good supply of mattresses, if not they're making the drawer their home, for their own homes elsewhere. Bread bins seem like an obvious and practical place to store bread but many types are not rodent proof, and the remains of crumbs invariably stay there for ages. If you do get a bread bin try to get an actual bin with a tight-fitting lid and not a flap designed one. Make a habit of tapping out old breadcrumbs for your neighbour's chickens each time a new loaf is put in.

Keep plastic bags stored in a container with a sealed top: plastic is a favourite bedding material, especially with the added bonus of traces of food still left in the bags. Not good tactics for putting mice off from coming in. Bedrooms are another good place to find bedding, naturally; it's a bedroom! But not just for us, men and mice alike want the best for their homes and beds. Look in the bedroom drawers and wardrobe shelves, as sometimes the mice gain entry from the back of the furniture, where the material is maybe just hardboard or plywood, easily nibbled for entry. Mice can squeeze through the minutest gaps, and using filler to seal them can reduce the risk; a necessity in the case of many Bulgarian-style rooms.

I've used all sorts of traps in Bulgaria: they don't work. In my opinion they're never sensitive enough, precarious to use and quite often just attract the mice, who whip the bait off the trap and come back the next day looking for more! Used outside, they catch hedgehogs, sparrows and other non-vermin creatures, but never mice. All these procedures may still not guarantee your house will be mouse-free, and that's where the trump card comes into play. Poison!

Place mouse poison at all times in places where mice would tend to investigate. Under kitchen drawers, behind fridges and freezers and right at the back of food cupboards at ground level in the kitchen. In the bedrooms, under the bed, behind wardrobes and in dressing tables — the list goes on. In my garage I use a couple of heavy Bulgarian slates leaning against the wall with the poison behind them. They cannot be moved by cats and are solely accessible to the vermin. This was also done in the barn where the hay and straw is kept, the bait checked once a week and topped up if necessary, and it works for me. But there will always be other vermin on their search for suitable places to live.

SIMPLE TREASURE - 11

- Skalitsa Maestros -

In Skalitsa getting something done simply, without any fuss, is impossible. In fact I would conclude that this applies to the whole of Bulgaria. We were spending another weekend on the farm, catching up on farm chores that had built up, compounded by the heavy rain during the week; it was going to be a busy time. No time for guests or relaxing; the weeds had bolted and the growth on the vegetables meant that extra supports had to be administered to support the tomatoes, peppers and to redirect the pumpkins, which had now decided to sprint into the other vegetables' domains and were in the process of strangling them! Because of the heavy rain and wind some plaster had come away from part of the main farmhouse building, and the outside wall needed to be re-plastered. Now these are things I avoid, mainly because I know nothing of plastering: I don't even know what is involved in mixing up plaster. I do know that the components are cement, sand and water, but the quantities are a mystery. After this day I was to become that much wiser, not just in knowing a bit more about it, but in keeping my mouth shut!

Galia, my Bulgarian girlfriend, knew more than I did about plastering, and she went about surveying the damage. It wasn't much, perhaps half a square metre that needed to be seen to. Being in Skalitsa, and on a Saturday, meant that material might be hard to come by, so it was friends and neighbours in Skalitsa that needed to be called upon. Galia said they were bound to have some materials to hand, as is always the case: nothing is wasted here, and leftover cement and sand would have been stored in outhouses for future use by every household —

guaranteed! I knew this was never going to be a case of simply getting the materials and getting advice on how to mix to make the plaster, and I knew for certain I wouldn't be allowed to do the work myself! Oh how I knew this....

It was going to be a job that would take a day, and as the saying goes, 'In Bulgaria you are lucky to get one job done in a day!' So off I went to my neighbour Sasho's to ask where materials and know-how could be found. It became his mission to get the job done, and some clattering could be heard as he entered his old garage, which used to hold a Lada (now sold to the Roma for metal). Clatter, clatter, bang, clatter; then silence. Silence is always more noticeable after a spell of noise, and out of the now very apparent silence a slight creak sounded from the rusted hinges as the big wooden garage door swung open and Sasho appeared, carrying a bucket full of sand. It looked very much like shingle; my first thought was about this being put on my wall, and how it would never match the existing texture. Then I thought about the Bulgarian mentality, and how fashion and style don't really come into play when DIY repairs are done; it's based purely on practicality and whatever repair material happens to be around at the time in the *maestro* world of Bulgaria — worrying times for nobody but me.

So the sand was here; where would the cement come from? Off we went to the local shop, where a round of questioning began; in particular of one Roma chap who seemed to have a lead — as they always do if there's a business opportunity or a possible money-making scenario. He knew of a source of cement from a house not too far away, and was apparently rewarded with a beer. Off we went, but not before getting a couple of plastic bags from behind the counter courtesy of Maria, the shop owner. Nearly two hours had gone by and the morning was drawing to an end as we reached a Roma house in a fair state of disrepair: flimsy bits of material as curtains for the doors and windows, no glass or wood in sight. I found it very strange that we were to come here for cement, as quite obviously the house hadn't seen repairs for many a year. Why would there be cement here?

Eventually a Roma man came out, looking as though he'd been asleep for a thousand years; his thick black hair standing up from being slept on and the whiff of alcohol oozing out invading the fresh country air and straight up our noses. He stumbled his way towards us. A few comments were exchanged and we were on our way to another house — another false rumour, and that previous Roma got a beer in Maria's shop for nothing! A hundred metres further on and well upwind from the intoxicating stench of alcohol-man another Bulgarian home was called upon. The small, fluffy, white but well-voiced dog was calling the owner well before we reached the gate of the immaculate house. We chatted for a while, and it became clear that cement was here, but that wasn't enough for the owner. He was apparently a maestro in plastering terms, and after hearing of the dilemma of the Englishman had now joined the party on a mission to sort out the problem. So now a very heavy bag of cement, which I wasn't allowed to carry as I was English, was taken from his very well organised workshop. On the way back we met another maestro, who professed that he knew better than they did regarding plastering; now he joined an ever-growing convoy of maestros on the way back to my place.

But that wasn't the case — first it was back to the shop and a sit down. The Roma who had freeloaded a beer had gone. We spent thirty minutes talking about the job in hand and concluded that now wasn't a good time. Three factors led to that decision: it was lunchtime, it was hot, so we should tackle the job this evening and last but most importantly, this is Bulgaria! It was now my turn to talk, as I insisted on paying for the materials and furthermore on doing the job myself. They had given away the information I needed to do this; specifically, that you need a ratio of 3:1 for the sand and cement. The insisting on my part fell on deaf ears, as I was not considered a maestro, and the considered plan of action was for the Bulgarian maestros to meet at my home that evening. So it was now midday; all the materials had been gathered, 'know how' had been passed on and the wait was now on for cooler conditions.... Half a day gone, but at least some progress had been made.

Jessica the doorbell dog sounded off at just gone 6:00 that evening, as Sasho turned up with the same bucket that was previously filled with gravel, but now I find that it is full of sand! He explained that he graded it by using a sieve that looked like a stretcher they bring onto football field to carry off injured footballers (or non-injured Italian footballers). Moments later Jessica sounded off again — two maestros had turned up with a friend. I wasn't quite sure whether he was a maestro too, but the chances were he was. So there were now five men, myself included, ready for the job of covering half a square metre patch of wall. I knew what was to happen next! Sasho started the business as the rest of us watched. He used my wheelbarrow to make the mix, working slowly and methodically. He added a bit of washing-up liquid with the mix, on the advice of one of the maestros, apparently so that the cement was easier to mix. Good or bad tip I don't know, but it was added, after much debate of course.

Galia was working full-time providing refreshments. It was hard work watching, after all, but that's how it's done here. The next stage was to rid the wall of loose debris and spray on some water to help the cement to stick. Solely, Sasho, with advice and pointing coming in from all angles, also did this. A little pause as more debate ensued, before the maestro who provided the cement now took over the waiting mixture. He had his maestro tool with him, and started slapping the cement in the areas it was needed, but not before checking the consistency of the mixture again, adding a little more water to it. Four of us were still looking on as the maestro told them to stop with the continuing advice that was coming from lesser maestros. Ten minutes later the job was complete. A nice smooth finish — in complete contrast to the speckled finish of the rest of the wall, but this did not bother the Bulgarians present, who all stood back to admire the work that had been done.

How on earth could I complain? The whole things hadn't cost me a stotinki; I hadn't even lifted a finger to help, in fact it felt more like I had been in the way! The trouble now was that they had spotted other areas of my wall that needed repair, and my garden patio was in dire need of being re-cemented. I didn't have a say in the matter, as they planned to do this the next week, and were already organising more cement and sand supplies to be brought in from Yambol. Another Bulgarian trait was leaving a mess! We appreciated the help, but it took longer to clear up the mess than it took to repair the wall. But as I say, how on earth can you complain? Could I have done this myself in the first place? Well, no, but I could now, with the experience of so many maestros and advice all the way along. In Skalitsa everyone is a maestro in everything, but some are better equipped than others in certain areas. If I were a typical British expatriate with British expectations I would probably be up in arms about the difference in finish compared to the rest of the wall, but I'm not.

SIMPLE TREASURE - 12

- In Bulgaria? You'll Do This Soon! -

Once you have been in Bulgaria for a while you will find yourselves picking up Bulgarian habits; some of them will probably have been taken on board without you even realising it. There are two reasons why you find these habits are taken on. The first is quite simply you copy the Bulgarians. After a while you don't understand why on earth you didn't do this years ago as they make so much practical sense. Secondly, these habits creep in subconsciously without you realising it, unless you are living in a 'Little Britain' society in Bulgaria and close your eyes to foreign things. Listed here are a few habits for starters:

- Wearing different sets of clothes for different situations is a must! One for the village, one for town and work, another for going out in the evening, and in the winter a different set of clothing for bed!
- Leaving food on your plate when you've had enough rather, than having to finish it up like a good boy.
- Walking fast just never happens now — it's taken a while to get to this stage though.
- Looking at my watch. Well, I don't wear one now — what's the point in knowing what time it is in Bulgaria?
- Ending a conversation — very difficult!
- Getting a job finished. There's always tomorrow, next week, next month, next year or in some cases waiting for your own reincarnation to finish it.
- Getting your Bulgarian friends to spend some time away from their GSMs (mobile phones). Impossible.

- Washing up or cleaning the home — THIS IS DEFINITELY NOT ALLOWED FOR MEN!
- Adjusting and enjoying rakia and salad every single evening, all year round. Actually I don't know how I managed to do cope without this before living here.
- Not looking before crossing a road: Tufty and the Green Cross Code Man have never been heard of or set foot in Bulgaria!

Not necessarily the top ten, but there's many more where they come from…..

SIMPLE TREASURE - 13

- Bulgarian Weather Talk -

It may seem a strange thing to say but it seems that the weather is talked about in Bulgaria more than I remember it being talked about in the UK! Bulgarian weather is the number one topic here. You would think in the villages, where farmers' crops depend on the weather, that the topic would be discussed more than in the towns and cities, but this is not the case; it applies to the whole country. It's a Bulgarian obsession to comment on the weather wherever they are — even to the point of commenting on the weather elsewhere in Bulgaria if there is nothing to say about the weather in their own area. On the rare occasions that the whole country has non-descript weather that doesn't rate much discussion they talk about the weather they had previously, or the weather that they are going to get, or even the weather they haven't had or won't get!

The weather in Bulgaria is also very regional. With the great diversity of land different climates are experienced, from the Northern Balkan mountain range down to the Thracian plains and the influence of the Black Sea in the east. So there can be more than three very different types of weather in three different places in Bulgaria at the same time. Regardless of the endless comment and discussion on weather, this is where the similarity ends compared with the UK. Whatever the weather in Bulgaria there is a very casual way of dealing with it; things carry on as normal, as with most things here. The weather doesn't 'get to them' in Bulgaria, as it is accepted very much as 'this is the weather we get, so what's the problem'! I recall working on the land one day in my village when some serious dark storm clouds gathered overhead; there was I running around like a headless chicken, putting things away, gathering up the hay that had been freshly cut earlier in the day so it could be covered with a plastic sheet before the rain came. Around me there were others working out on the fields; as I looked up they had all stopped working, not due to the inbound weather but just to look at me running around like a mad dog!

The downpour came — as I said it, doesn't mess around, and the heavens opened. The hot Bulgarian sun returned after a short while, drying everything out in the same amount of time it took me to cover everything before the rains came. Bulgarian folk looking on were wondering what all the fuss had been about, and why I had wasted my energy. In fact it was a distraction from the current weather talk. It seems like a strange contradiction, to act so casually about their weather yet talk about it so much. The only way I can sum up the contradiction is where you may get two Bulgarians talking about the rainy weather — in the rain! If you want to get involved in the community here in Bulgaria it is very useful to learn some Bulgarian words and phrases about the weather. This goes down very well in casual conversation and is a valuable tool to have, to be used on almost every occasion you meet people here.

SIMPLE TREASURE - 14

- Bulgarian Village Life — A Glimpse -

I got another glimpse of Bulgarian village life today as my neighbour for some two years now starts another day. He is also now my honorary brother, as he often reminds me. Today however, he has me with him for a few hours. He knows I write about everything I do here and is fully aware that another article will be written about what I see and do here this morning. In fact he is quite proud, but at the same time I know that he will not change his normal routine with this knowledge. This man, Sasho, is the kindest gentlest person you could imagine. Sasho was born in 1954. He tells me this on every occasion, and the date of his birthday. At well over six feet tall and as thin as a stick, he has protruding lips, which are his main feature, and a variety of scabs on his almost bald head from various Bulgarian doorways that he has misjudged. He is naturally clumsy in unfamiliar surroundings, but amazingly agile, skilful and confident when dealing with matters out of doors and smallholding chores.

He and his wife make a very weather-beaten couple, complementing each other with that distinct look of Bulgarian country folk. This is a look that is very different from the Bulgarian people from towns and cities. On the odd occasion they visit the town this difference is pronounced — even though they dress in their best outfits for such events, they just don't fit into town style or town life. That is not to say Rosa, his wife, doesn't like the town; Sasho hates it, but Rosa, like most Bulgarian women, glimpses the other life and is naturally drawn to the fashion that is around, something that just wasn't there a few years ago. The feeling is that Rosa knows deep down that it is now too late in life for her to change her village ways, but she doesn't feel sorry for herself. She considers her life a happy one and is just as happy for the younger generation. This includes her own children, who she sees enjoying the modern freedom and liberalism.

The only reason Rosa, Sasho and other people go to town is to pay yearly bills or to buy medicine for the farm animals. In fact it is quite a chore for them, as they have to play catch-up in the village when they get back. They go less often now, as I regularly shop on their behalf, saving the lugging on the bus and the one kilometre walk from the bus stop. In fact the orders have gone up recently, due to the cheaper cost of provisions such as chicken feed in the town. These people are as poor as church mice but they live very comfortably, in a smallholding that is not quite at the point of falling down but has been kept in order in a very Bulgarian way. Interestingly enough, last year part of Sasho's outbuilding collapsed; it was only used for storing hay for the winter, but instead of being upset he was pleased, as the tiles, bricks and wood were now available for use on other repair projects, and he now has fuel for the wood burner. There were still two thirds left of the outbuilding, so next year the hay will just be stacked higher!

Roof leaks aren't fixed but redirected by placing a bit of metal beneath the offending tiles. Guttering that in places jutted out from the eaves was fixed originally in the wrong place as the pace of the water that runs down the pitch of the roof throws it beyond the gutter gully and bypasses the whole drainage system. Downpipes are used more by rats than rain, with the waterfalls running parallel to them in heavy downpours. I have lost count of the number of times I have helped bail out their ground floor living area, not from rain from the sky but from the underground water that comes a day after heavy rain, welling up from the saturated ground. I always get the call in the evening for me to turn up the next day for this routine. They can't or don't know how to solve this problem with nature, but just deal with it when it happens. Strangely, winter isn't the worst time for this, for two reasons: they live on the first floor in the winter, when the rain is usually more constant. The rain that had fallen during the day usually freezes in the extreme sub-zero temperatures overnight. The next day the frozen water will slowly defrost and trickle away with a little warm winter sun.

The house, as I say, looks in a state of disrepair to the western eye, and in need of a complete overhaul and renovation. Yes, it is a shambolic looking house, but a comfortable enough home for these kind Bulgarians. It was a shock when I was first invited in, but as time went along I learned that it is really is a lived-in house, with the warmth of the family more than enough to make it far more homely than many a renovated western-styled home. Many times people have said to me, 'Why don't you get air conditioners?', 'Why don't you build a wall to make your yard completely private?', 'Why don't you sleep in the bedroom instead of the living room?' If you have lived in Bulgaria for any length of time and have taken to living the Bulgarian way, this answers many of these and other questions. In fact my own house was very much influenced by my Bulgarian neighbours; the British design and layout of my house and grounds just didn't work, neither in the winter nor in the summer. It's yet another aspect of the Bulgarian way of thinking and living that has had a major influence on my own thinking since coming here.

These were people who had brought up two children, a son and a daughter who now have left the fold to work in the city — there just isn't work in the village. How often do you see this happening in Bulgaria? Will they come back when their parents are too old to cope? Well, this question was asked, and the answer was a resounding 'No', but they love their time here on the occasions that they visit. As time goes by, childhood memories become more vivid — will this happen here? Will they want to come back and recapture their childhood memories in the village of their ancestors, and slow down from the pace of city, or is it just Brits who pine for this retro life?

It was 5:30 with the orange sun already over the brow of the mountain in the distance and clearing its throat of the thinnest of hazes for what looked like a day of profuse sweating ahead. Having experience of working on my own farm and the great variety each day holds, it was with mild curiosity I looked forward to the differences in Sasho's working day. Many a time I would help him out tackling some jobs, just as he often helped me, but these were in isolation, a single snapshot from the day's roll of film.

The stereo doorbells, two of them either side of the house, gave an antiphonal effect, with piercing yaps and yelps; yes, they are dogs! And enough to wake the dead anywhere else, but Sasho is apparently unstirred by the alarm call. There was a clear sky and a full moon the previous night, and the wolves in the nearby forest were in full cry, prompting all the dogs in the area to join in with their distant relatives for a monthly ensemble of canine counterpoint. A log would have been proud of me as

I slept last night; perhaps Sasho had had a bad night, being the last house in the village and the closest to the packs of full-throttled, moonlight-powered lamb-eating wolves!

Half past five. There was a sound of shuffling paper round the back of the house. I don't often go there, but I know what it is. The small building situated there is like the little biscuit home of that evil witch in the Hansel and Gretel fairy story, with its brightly-coloured orange roof and gaudy red, yellow and green of the door, window and hanging toilet roll respectively. In fact the yellow toilet roll was on a small black painted log, looking just like one of those liquorice allsorts! The shuffling sound suddenly painted a different picture in my mind, knowing that it was coming from inside the toilet! Moments later the door moved and Sasho emerged with a big smile, showing his one remaining tooth. The other one had been removed the previous week, which was when he ate his last ever salted chick pea. We normally shake hands 'Rasta style', as we are brotherhood now, but this didn't happen as he made his way to the outside tap to wash his hands. You know they do this often by the wear on the soap. One thing that remains constant for many, but not all Bulgarians, is the sense of hygiene they practice. This is always the sign of a respectable family and quite often this is a fair way of judging Bulgarians, and basically a good indicator of how well educated they are. The same applies in the UK, I'm sure!

Sasho put his hands in the air, gesturing towards the sun, saying 'Toplo Den!' ('It's a hot day!'). With his straw cowboy hat, traditional village blue top and matching blue dungarees, below which were the thickly knitted socks in his cut-away rubber sandals and village features built in, he looked the part. And an exact replica was standing by him, in the same well-worn outfit from top to bottom, with perhaps more cut away from the sandals, but somehow it wasn't the same; for a moment I felt like a counterfeit and an impostor. All geared up for work, we walked to the chicken patch. There were around fifty of them, half for eggs and half for the year's supply of meat. Their food and water was topped up and two eggs gathered and brought inside. Only two? Well, if you know chickens they lay most eggs between nine and two, so more gathering would be done later. This only took around five minutes, and as we took the two eggs and returned to the house Rosa was telling us to come into the summerhouse.

This is the downstairs room, basically a bed-sit kitchen and the coolest place for the hottest seasons. The TV was on with Bulgarian pop-folk blasting away, and a table full of food. There were pancakes, fresh bread, white cheese, ayran yoghurt drink in a big jug beside three tall glasses all standing to attention. In addition there was homemade salami from the pig slaughtered last Christmas and shimmering hot coffee. So, five minute's work done and the eating begins. Whether this is done regularly I don't know — there's a strong possibility that my presence is a licence to feast, as most Bulgarians I know start the day with coffee and a cigarette on the toilet! Not today. Thirty minutes had now gone by and the TV music, talking, eating and finishing off the ayran was still in progress. The reason that was given all the time was fuel for work! Little did they know, and it wouldn't have made any difference if they did, that I'd eaten a full breakfast half an hour before! My insistence that we get on with the routine of the day finally paid off as Rosa started to move some of the cutlery. Of course I have known for a very long time now that any offer of help would have driven Rosa and Sasho to give me looks that would have turned me to stone twice over! I was a man, and this is not what men do here! We moved off, leaving Rosa to do her Bulgarian woman thing. I was sure it wouldn't be too long before we were back at the table with a fresh spread.

It was after six in the morning now, and we went out to inspect the goats. There were three adults, and seven kids who were old enough to do their own thing; these were let out to roam the semi-enclosed area outside the house boundary and the adults, all female, with milk almost bursting from their udders, we milked. It is normal that the surplus milk is sold for forty stotinki a litre to the local cooperative store. But today the surplus wasn't going there — it was given to me as payment for helping! What do I do with four litres of goat milk? Before, knowing what to do with this much would have been hard; now it's no problem, I have so many options in my head for using it. I have no goats, other than the one that I put in the freezer last month, so goat's milk was a bonus today. The milk was strained and bottled, and I took my share back to my house a hundred metres down the road and into the fridge for later. The goats joined the other village goats with the shepherd at around 7:15, and we were free to muck out the goat pen.

Most of these chores are done solely by Sasho, but it takes longer when I am there as he has someone to talk to and we stop every so often to do just that. It is quite strange, but looking at all the chores to be done seems like a major job in itself, and a mild panic sets in contemplating about how long it will take. Sasho thinks very differently: he takes things so slowly and gently, like a little mouse nibbling away. He often pauses to look around, and sometime squats down in a yogic fashion to light and smoke a cigarette, but never stops talking. The talking only stops on occasions when a little run of work takes place, but it is not long before this tall, thin man strikes up another cigarette and conversation at the same time. 8:00. The sun is now quite high in the sky and the searing heat begins; it is time for a break. It has felt like a morning stroll so far, and as we approach the summerhouse I can smell the coffee and hear the TV still on. We all sit again for another thirty minutes, with coffee and another round of sweet bread that Rosa had cooked while we were out! It is quite a worry, this man's smoking habits: he gets through forty a day, eighty between him and Rosa, but they never get out of breath. The reason is clear: they never work fast enough to aerobically tax their lungs.

My few hours had finished by 9:00 and the chores were now waiting at my own smallholding. I asked if one day I could spend the whole day with him, bring along my camera, and write about it later. They were both very excited about the camera, and of course they didn't mind, it was something different for them when I was there, not that they get bored at all with what they do. Just these few hours gave an insight into the laid back ways of these through-and-through country folk, and I feel very fortunate to be their neighbour and honorary brother. All the little things I notice about life here seem very different from where I came from. Could I imagine doing this day in day out until I die? Well, at almost fifty years of age now, and very fit, I have throughout my life had a variety of experiences trying to reach a goal. The trouble has always been not knowing what that goal was. Having now reached this point in life I feel that I am closer to that goal than I have ever been.

SIMPLE TREASURE - 15

- Litterbugs -

Rubbish in Bulgaria is all around, and this is the strong and quite off-putting first impression many visitors get. This has been put down to a hangover after the communist era, where you could be arrested and impounded for dropping litter in the street; what a good idea! Since the demise of communism part of the freedom included the right to litter the streets without any fear of recriminations, and because they now have this right they exercise it to the full. This is more in retaliation to the previous system, and has now become embedded in countless Bulgarians who could be quite simply described as litterbugs. The trouble is that the habits of the parents get passed on to the next generation and right now what I see is confusion in littering habits. Yes, the schools do teach ideals of caring for the community you live in, but a mixed message is coming from their parents.

The reason for towns and cities being 'clean' is mainly due to the street cleaners. If you rise early before the streets have been given a going over you will see rubbish scattered everywhere; dogs, cats and whatever other animals are around have been into the big bins, leaving a mayhem of litter on the road and pavements. Included in the scavenging the previous evening are the Roma, who sift through the wastage for cardboard, plastic and metal for patching up their homes, selling on or fuel material for cooking and/or heating. In the countryside, the designated fields for waste are used in the main, but many fly tip their rubbish on the side of roads, and even in areas right next to the tips. There is no resolution to comply with the very loose rules laid down for these assigned tips. Bulgarians seem to think it is their right to fly tip. After all, look at all the space we have outside the towns — what's the problem? That's the thinking here, and after the weather deals out some high winds, the whole countryside looks like a panoramic landfill. The main culprits in this voyage of waste are plastic bags, which have a natural nomadic urge, never being content with their first landing spot.

Back in the towns you can see Roma children regularly searching through bins especially in town centre fast food joints. They pick out left over food then walk off, eating what they've found. This is quite common here, and a shock at first sight, but all part of how Bulgaria functions on a day-to-day basis. This is quite a contradiction to the Roma who litter more than the Bulgarians. You can almost certainly recognise most Roma homes by the litter that surround them; this is just how they are here in Bulgaria, using their surroundings, including their own yards and 'gardens' as rubbish dumps. Things will change gradually with the introduction of on-the-spot fines, conforming with EU policy, and in fact a throwback to communist times. This time around though the punishment, as always in this increasingly westernised society, will be financial penalties. It must be said that for many visitors to Bulgaria the litter spread around the country is quite an off-putting factor, and even now an annoyed 'tut tut' is made when seeing Bulgarian folk thrown litter down without a thought. Perhaps this is one aspect of Bulgaria that doesn't appeal to the foreigner; Bulgarians of course deem this as normal and socially acceptable. How can a population brought up on conservation and green living behave in this way?

SIMPLE TREASURE - 16

- The Bulgarian Door -

A bit about the Bulgarian door. Fifty years or more, that's how old this Bulgarian door was on my newly renovated house in Skalitsa. I know this because my house was built in the same year I was born, and came with the door. It was a main focal point that people saw on arrival and a major talking point for many a guest of mine. As the only entry point to the house it had been opened to thousands of other guests and closed in the face of unwelcome members of the community in its time. Since buying my farmhouse everything had been replaced in the renovation except the wooden front door and the internal doors, all of which have such history and character.

The suggestion that the front door should be turned into a new aluminium PVC version had been made not only by expatriate friends and family but also from local Bulgarians. These Bulgarians have no qualms or sentiments about losing a part of the heritage of a house when it comes to practicality: this wins hands down every time. The door was ill-fitting and the only security in place was a metal catch that swivelled across, no more than 5 cm in length. It did stop the door from rattling in the wind, but that was the limit of its function. The arched windows at the top were of a glass off-cut style, held in place by a couple of tacks but not sealed in between the joins. The various multi-patterned frosted windows had been recycled from other buildings at some point. The air flowed freely through the gaps; no need for a cat flap, as the space between the bottom of the door and the floor was enough, if not for a kitten, certainly for a rat! I loved my door. There was something about this door that I didn't want to let go of. It had been through two winters with me. The big thick curtain that hung in from of the door stopped the elements getting in, and it felt Bulgarian and cosy. During the summer the door was tied back to the adjoining wall, kept fully open for superb ventilation through the interior homemade mesh door.

As always in Bulgaria these things all worked, and I really didn't see the need to have it replaced. Am I really British? Why change my mind? My neighbour recently had his front door renovated — it was stripped of decades-old layers of paint, had a couple of new panels added, then finished off in clear varnish. The finished product was impressive for a Bulgarian door. This sowed the seed in my partner Galia's mind — she was determined to get me to change my door, and a plan was formulating. The plan: the decision was made to get a replacement door, not to renovate the old one. I was quite upset in one sense, but again the practicality of a new aluminium door was overwhelmingly favoured, although the security factor hardly mattered around here! I was going to make inquiries with a building company in Yambol town, but was scorned by the locals, who had now taken the matter into their own hands. I had no control over what I wanted, and knew there would be trouble ahead. I think it was due the fact that there was an aluminium window and door factory based in my home village of Skalitsa that compelled the locals to get the business done there. Not only that, but they offered a fitting service as well. So the door was measured up, ordered and a date set to fit it. Goodbye fair door, you served us well.

Saturday arrived and the morning brought two chaps from the factory with the door in hand. After just an hour the place was shrouded in dust, splinters and rubble as the men said goodbye. Goodbye!? Are they off to lunch, or what? Surely they can't leave things as they are? They can and did. I was livid — the door was standing in absolute clutter and chaos, and I was standing in total disbelief. Call that a job? Now Galia, being Bulgarian, just couldn't understand why I was so upset; the door was fitted, what was the problem? As I explained, there was exposed brickwork all around and more cat flaps in the seals of foam that were slowly hardening. Much of the plaster on the adjoining wall had come away, leaving a door that apparently could be blown down in the wind. My treasured old door and homemade fly screen door were carefully stored away before we started clearing all the mess the door installers had left. After an hour or so it looked just as bad; the door now the highlight without the distraction of clutter. Next step? We needed a plasterer, and we needed one now, as we were due back in Yambol the next day and the place wasn't secure. Oh, how I wished we had got that British building company to do the work — it would have been completely serviceable by now, and we could have spent the rest of the weekend relaxing.

We reckoned we would have to tour all the cafes and bars of the village, but fortunately found a plasterer in the first one we visited. Good job we caught him before he ended up getting plastered himself. (We were to find out later that he didn't drink *or* smoke, as it happens.) He said he was the only one that could do the job now, although there are around four hundred plasterers in Skalitsa, they really aren't hard to find. We had no materials and had to find the owner of the hardware store, who was drinking in another bar (he did drink and smoke). He went back to his shop with us and opened up especially for us to buy the cement and plaster for the job. It was Saturday afternoon, with a very hot and bothered Englishman ferrying around this supposed Skalitsa *maestro* in the pursuit of tools and materials for the job. The weekend gone! We finally got what we needed, and the job commenced well into the mid-afternoon. The guy seemed to know what he was doing, and left our house at ten that evening after we had fed and watered him. He did a good job as far as I could see; re-cementing the demolition job beforehand and finishing off with plaster, but it wasn't finished. He was to return at nine on Sunday morning to complete the job — so much for a relaxing weekend for Gal and me. Not only did he finish the job, he also went around the rest of the porch repairing cracks and badly-sealed plaster, then went indoors to do the same in every room.

It was now four in the afternoon and all finished, but as usual the mess left was horrendous, and another two hours were spent cleaning at high speed, as we had to be back in Yambol before dark. Looking back before we departed, we both examined the work that had been done; apart from the door it wasn't clinical by any means, with its typical Bulgarian-style contours of wavering walls. Yes, it retained some of old Bulgaria in its shape and style, but if I were any other British expatriate with British expectations I would not be happy with the result and have the thing done all over again. Another Bulgarian maestro he may be, but that would rather devalue the word maestro to many outsiders. Would I have wished I'd had the job done by a British-managed and British-standardised company? For me, with my Bulgarian partner and friends knowing what to expect, I am forced to say no. I am here to live, totally immersed in the Bulgarian community, and if that's how things are done here, no matter how badly from a foreign eye, then that's what I accept. I understand fully the expectations of many who come here and the standard of work wanted. Doing it my way, Bulgarian style, may work for me but for anyone else, you have been warned! Don't expect a job to be done the way you want it to be done by employing local workers; you will be setting yourselves up for a nightmare scenario. At the end of the day the Bulgarian door now is still a Bulgarian door, made in Skalitsa and fitted by Skalitsa folk in Bulgarian style — never going to be perfect, but that's Bulgaria!

SIMPLE TREASURE - 17

- Tarator Recipe -

Tarator is a legendary albeit very simple dish, a bit like a cold soup. It's often made as a cooling snack during the warmer weather, when the ingredients are always in good supply. Occasionally it is served as a treat in the winter.

Ingredients (serves 4):

- 1 litre full fat yoghurt
- 2 medium cucumbers
- 10-12 walnuts
- 1 cup sunflower oil
- fresh dill
- 1 medium garlic bulb

Preparation:

Finely chop the cucumbers, walnuts, dill and garlic. Mix all the ingredients and put in the fridge to cool for at least an hour. Ladle the tarator into chilled soup bowls.

Note: The quantities of the ingredients can be increased or decreased to your own personal taste.

SIMPLE TREASURE - 18

- Healing Stones – More Evidence! -

It was August; the schools were closed, giving a well-earned break for many teachers and their families in the UK. There we were in Skalitsa, not having seen two sets of very good friends for a number of years, and wouldn't you know it they both decided to call upon me during the same week! We managed to stagger their visits to the farmhouse, then we went about showing off our Bulgarian village and how wonderful life is here. The first couple were an old school friend (a rock 'n' roll entertainer and part-time school caretaker) and his future wife, who was a head teacher. Both were full of the stresses from work, added to which were the aches and pains that appear approaching the big five oh. The journey to Skalitsa is a long one — from London to the Midlands to get the flight, then another four hours from Sofia to Yambol before being picked up and transported to Skalitsa — but this was August, and the only travel avenue open if you don't book early.

Both our guests were in a strange place, without much sleep, with many hours of talking and catching up on news. However, some homegrown salad and homemade sliva rakia did help a bit! The next morning the lack of sleep showed as we walked the short distance to the healing stones, not only to test the remedy for aching bodies, but also as an experiment in their curative properties for hangovers. We lay there for some twenty minutes and let the stones do their stuff, and do you know, the hung over feeling disappeared in a very short space of time. There was a spring in our step as we walked down the hill towards the bar just five minutes away for a coffee. These good friends of mine were stunned into silence in the strong Skalitsa sun, confessing that it was like having their batteries recharged and joints oiled. We then walked to a local reservoir, and after admiring Alex and Julia, the two ostriches, on the bank we took a paddleboat out on the mirrored waters. These friends were still stunned at the beauty of the whole area, and swore to return here for therapeutic effects they now believe the rocks possess.

With the first friends despatched to the Black Sea coast, full of energy, I fetched my other friends, a college lecturer and his new wife, a professional viola player. They were still on their honeymoon! She in particular has many problems with her shoulder that come as part of her vocation, and is common with many viola players, myself included until my recent healing by the stones. After a good night's sleep we took our viola-playing friend to the rocks, and as she lay there next to Galia she didn't want to leave. The warmth of the rocks just felt so comfortable, especially with the knowledge that they may cure. Eventually we wandered back down the hill to visit St. George's, Skalitsa's 150-year old church, full of treasures. Back in my farmhouse she commented that she felt as though she had been asleep for days and was completely refreshed; no reoccurring twinges in her bowing shoulder, and fully fit for the rest of the vacation here. We received more comments on how beautiful the countryside is here and how lucky we were to live here. It never fails to amaze me that all who have been to visit the stones have come away from them at the very least full of life, and more often than not free of previous aches and pains — now including hangovers! As for me, one year on and my shoulder still feels as good as new; two more bursts of the magnetic powers from the healing stones this last week should continue to add to the evidence.

SIMPLE TREASURE - 19

- Bulging Bulgarian Buses -

I was without the Lada car one weekend, so I returned to using the bus from Yambol to Skalitsa and back again. This is something I used to do regularly but haven't for quite a while, and I looked forward to the experience once again. One thing I noticed was that the fare had remained the same as it was two years ago: three leva each way for the 35 km trip. The difference now was that a minibus was used instead of the old-fashioned coach, which I'd had the pleasure of using in the past. These were vehicles so full of character that they should have had names: Boris the Bus, or Kristina the Coach. It is such a shame that they are being decommissioned. There are still a few about, but not on our route today. The trip to Skalitsa was typical for a Friday evening and the last trip of the day — packed to the hilt! Many passengers who hadn't forced their way to the front of the queue just had to stand in a bunch. There was no fear of falling over as the rolling minibus negotiated the pot-holed town roads — they were packed so closely together they couldn't move, let alone fall over. We were lucky: Galia was Bulgarian, and furthermore a Bulgarian woman, and she employed her skilful Bulgarian technique of pushing to the front, then saving a place for me once on the bus. I still can't bring myself to do such things, with the 'ladies first' culture still embedded in me.

It was a stuffy journey but we had only a short walk to my farm — the driver took us almost to our doorstep, as the bus drivers do over here. The journey back on Sunday afternoon was yet another experience that sticks in my mind, and something I had not encountered on this scale until now. The bus was due at 4:30, but didn't roll up until 5:00, which wasn't too surprising, as 4:30 is another way of saying 5:00 in Bulgaria! There were at least fifteen people waiting to get on, and it was already fully laden, including those who had been standing all the way from the town of Topolovgrad and all the villages en route! 'Should we resign ourselves to staying in Skalitsa for another night?' was my immediate thought, and I was quite willing to trade the crush on the bus for an early rise tomorrow morning. The other Bulgarians, including Galia, had no such thoughts. A crowd descended on the driver, GSMs went into overdrive, and moments later another minibus turned up; this one was empty and we duly boarded it. With more standing than seated, both minibuses crawled off in convoy. I knew that there were another three villages before Yambol, with more passengers waiting to be picked up, and we were travelling at full capacity already! How would they cope? Well, at the first village were another six or seven expectant passengers, and the shuffling towards the back of the bus started in earnest.

It was at this point that Galia and I started to realise that this was quite funny, but only because we had seats. If we hadn't been seated then our smiles would have been wiped off completely, especially as some of the standing population — now definitely cuddling against their will — weren't just glowing or perspiring, but sweating like horses! Another village, five more crammed on, and more shuffling back. I didn't think this was possible as the minibus, like a mobile can of sardines, moved off again at an even slower rate than before, and for good reason with the load it was now carrying. The last village was Roza, the biggest village and the biggest number of travellers wanting to board for Yambol. There were at least another ten wanting to step on; surely this was not possible?

More shuffling, and a further four passengers squeezed aboard. We could see there were people now sitting on each others' laps, and Galia sat on mine, freeing up another seat. Others, however, who didn't know each other, refused to do this. One child was then put on the driver's lap, and the remaining passengers sat on the boarding steps, leant into the contours of the front windscreen or sat on the side of the driver's dashboard!

All were now fitted together like a jigsaw puzzle and the bus had begun to move slowly off when suddenly there was a shout from the back! Someone had fallen asleep and had just woken up — he wanted to get off at Roza... Apart from those sitting on top of each other in seats, the whole bus had to disembark to let this old chap off, and then wedge themselves in as before. Despite all the hassle the atmosphere took a lift, as everyone saw the humorous side of the whole situation. The bus now approached Yambol and the roads were driven over very carefully, not least because of the child helping with the steering!

We arrived at the bus station to a certain air of disbelief that so many people could fit into a minibus. Another Bulgarian experience which could have been much worse if I hadn't been with Galia, who forced herself into a seat in the first place! The strange thing was that everyone seemed to accept that this happens, and made think that this is a regular situation for these travellers. What compounds matters even further are the mounds of luggage people take back to their apartments in the town, stuffed with all the produce they have grown in the villages — the minibuses having no provision for this. We were no exception, with three big carrier bags full of tomatoes, peppers etc. gathered from the farm. I would recommend this type of journey to anyone, purely so you can appreciate your current form of transport and having some degree of sympathy for Bulgarian travellers without cars.

SIMPLE TREASURE - 20

- Alternative Medicine in Bulgaria -

Alternative medicine is practiced all around the world, not least in Bulgaria where traditional remedies mixed with a little superstition are believed to work effectively as they have done through many generations. Bad luck, and the stress that comes with it, is a part of life no matter where you are, and it is dealt with in different ways. In Bulgaria there is alternative treatment, bordering on witch doctor magic. This is widely believed and practiced, and for the second time since living here I have found the need to visit the local practitioner in Skalitsa. It came to pass that some English guests had come to stay and we all caught a virus and were ill for three days. On top of this my Lada car had broken down and we had to use taxis. To complete a trilogy of disasters the car was smashed up on the way to the garage to be fixed. So the week of vacation left us totally drained from illness, the cost of taxi fares and now the cost of car repairs. The stress of the whole episode had got on top of us. We decided to travel to Skalitsa and get treatment for this the Bulgarian way.

Having gone through this procedure before it was familiar territory for me, and this time I knew what it was all about. This hadn't been the case first time around! Before, when taken there by my neighbour after crashing another car, I had not really known why, until some months afterwards when I had picked up a bit more of the Bulgarian language. As the appointment was made, we decided that as well as my partner and I our neighbour was to go, as she had found a snake in her kitchen that very morning. She had a phobia of them, resulting in a severely stressed Bulgarian woman who was in need of therapeutic help immediately.

We needed to take two leva each for the services, and a piece of lead; my neighbour managed to supply her own, as she had a Bulgarian fishing ledger weight that was still made from pure lead. My own fishing tackle, although the weights looked like real lead, was in fact made from another metal compound, lead weights having been banned in the UK for a number of years now, so we had to travel empty-handed in the hope that Maria, the healing doctor, had a supply to hand. Maria was ready for us when we arrived: a cylinder of bottled gas and a cooking plate supported a big tablespoon in the middle of her living room floor. Beside the gas cooker there was placed a small white bowl of water and a screw-topped plastic container, which held a supply of lead. We were in luck — the lead was in stock, and the treatment could start.

I was first in line, seated on the chair as some lead was dropped into the spoon and held over the intense heat. It wasn't long before the lead melted in the spoon, and with this the bowl of water was picked up and placed over my head. A chant was whispered and the spoon touched to three sides of the bowl before the lead was submersed, screeching as it hit the water. It was then placed back over the heat for re-melting, and the same process was performed twice more above my head. The treatment then moved onto the chest area: more chanting while tapping the edge of the bowl and the return of solid metal from the water. My legs got the final treatment, and at one point a sizzling piece of lead jumped out of the water, missing my bare foot by a couple of centimetres and scorching the rug on the floor. This rather shook me up, considering what could have happened! This was repeated four times, as the lower part of my body apparently had high stress levels. Each time the lead was picked out of the water it was examined, and the process repeated if the shape of the lead warranted another session in that particular area. It was clear from the shape that formed that there were problems in my lower body, hence the process being repeated again and again. Afterwards the now very warm water from the bowl that the lead had been in was transferred into a glass and I was asked to take three small sips. This I duly did, knowing that it was probably contaminated with lead, but this is Bulgaria and Bulgarian ways and traditions are respected.

Whilst Maria turned away to pour the water into the glass a payment of two leva was placed on the floor by the stove and was picked up whilst the sipping was going on. I remembered from before that the payment was made whilst neither party was looking. Galia was next, and no less than five submersions were done above her head; there were obviously problems there. My neighbour followed, as I observed, trying to study the shapes in the lead that caused the process to be repeated or to move on. It seemed that the lead definitely took on jagged and sharp characteristics in some areas, entailing further repetitions of the process, and a smoother finish when applied to presumably less-afflicted areas of the body. All were asked to take three sips of the water whilst the payments were being made, and then we were presented with our lumps of lead, wrapped in newspaper.

Because my partner still had problems with the lead over her head, a follow-up procedure was performed: Maria took a handful of salt crystals in her hand and, whispering another incantation, sprinkled some over her head. This was done at least three times before Maria was satisfied that the treatment had been effected. The wrapped-up lead was now to be placed under the pillow for three nights and then thrown into a river so the lead, now full of the owner's stress, would be washed downstream never to return. It is interesting that the Bulgarians truly believe in this practice, and part of its success is the unwavering belief in the process. This of course is another major contributing factor — that the process is actually working through psychological channels of suggestion.

SIMPLE TREASURE – 21

- A Sorry Dog Tale in Bulgaria -

This is a true but very sad story about British dog owners and Bulgarian country folk, with one loser at the end: the dog. A British couple had set up their dream home in a small, remote village in a farming community, very much like thousands of other villages scattered around the Bulgarian countryside. Livestock roaming the streets was commonplace in these areas; all calm, peaceful and living in harmony with the community. Traditional ways of keeping dogs in Bulgaria are very different to that of British ways and this primarily was the heart of the problem. The British couple remained adamant that their dog should live with them very much in the British fashion. It was allowed to run around the countryside, live and sleep in the house, and essentially be treated as part of the household. It would often be let out to roam free in the streets and fields outside the boundaries of the farmhouse grounds, and before long the sad saga began.

An elderly neighbour had called round to the house, complaining that the dog had attacked and killed many chickens from her farm, and blaming the British couple for letting the dog roam free. The matter was resolved simply, the old woman being compensated with money to replace the chickens and a promise from the British couple not to let the dog out unsupervised in the future. The dog was now confined within the boundaries of the farmhouse land, but still without being tethered. It was only a matter of time before it found escape routes out of the vast grounds and continued to chase and worry sheep, goats and poultry in the area. The livestock owners had full justification to continue to complain, but the couple remained firm about the dog being allowed its freedom, regardless of the stress it was causing to local livestock. The dog was apparently obedient when the owners were there, but not when they were absent.

Subsequently, with the owner absent on other occasions, more local chickens were killed and more monetary compensation was made, but this really wasn't the way forward as far as the Bulgarian locals were concerned. They were living in fear of the next attack, and the worrying was affecting milk production in the sheep and goats. Still the British couple refused to accept that their dog was not under control in their absence. They continued to insist that the dog should be unleashed at all times, even in their absence, and no compromise was sought, as they felt they were morally right in the way the dog should be brought up. No real regard was given to the loss of local Bulgarian livelihoods that were being caused by this dog.

This couldn't carry on: and so we come to the part that brought the matter to an end. The British owners were away again for a few days, and on their return they found that the dog had been poisoned and lay dead within their own grounds. The calculated consequence from the locals' point of view was that they had one less worry and their stocks were now safe. For the British couple there was now a feeling of bitterness and suspicion of many of their closest neighbours, and the house is now up for sale pending their move to another village. The mayor and local policeman were approached regarding the matter, but their response was a shrug of the shoulders; there was nothing they could or indeed would do about it! The question of who was right and who was wrong is raised, but some might say it was an inevitable end in Bulgaria.

SIMPLE TREASURE - 22

- Rakia Experiences -

Over the last few years the number of different types of rakia that I have tasted in Bulgaria may well have gone into three figures. The variety of rakia is astounding, not only in the variety of fruit bases used to make it, but in individual techniques, including innumerable secret family recipes. Rakia drinking has no fancy tasting practices associated with it, so it is not at all snobbish. It is the peoples' drink; a drink that has no prejudice and certainly no class boundaries, drunk by kings and peasants alike. It is usually consumed with a simple side salad, a sharp chink of glasses and a 'Nazdrave!' The beauty, the simplicity and the rewards of these moments are second to none. Salad, by the way, is all year round: cabbage throughout the winter, lettuce up until early summer, tomatoes, spring onions and cucumber from the spring through to the end of autumn. Of course shopska salad with the inclusion of sirene is always a more than pleasurable option. Incidentally potato salad is supposed to be accompanied by beer.

On the occasion I am offered a good quality single malt whisky, my taste buds now yearn for the rakia experience. I can honestly say that at this point the enjoyment of a good rakia now far outweighs the enjoyment of a good whisky by a long shot. This may be to do with the Bulgarian environment and company, alongside the lack of snob factor. Funnily enough the massive contrast in cost between the products does not have any bearing on this preference, although it's a massive incidental bonus!

Having said that, there have been many occasions where the quality of homemade rakia has been rough, to say the least, and there have been quite a few that stick in my mind. Naturally, their makers deem these the best in the village. It's funny, but even before you sample rakia you can usually tell what it is going to be like from knowing the people who have made it — the character of the rakia is usually a reflection of its maker. If you get a chance to see the process of rakia-making and distilling you'll never forget it. From a disgusting mix of slush to pure crystal-clear rakia is a remarkable transition. And the process doesn't stop there.... It never fails to amaze me that some of the fermented mixes, incorporating things that zoos would be proud of, turn out to have qualities that cannot be produced through legal commercial processes! The characteristics of these rakia are unique, and from my experience cannot be replicated by anyone other than Bulgarians, who seem to have a total disregard and seeming lack of understanding of the word 'hygiene'. This of course is not universal in Bulgaria, and just like everywhere else there are good and bad hygiene practices. That's one of the beauties of Bulgaria: the people in the villages who are not hamstrung by laws and regulations but rely on practical experience.

There is so much more to rakia than meets the eye, such as its medicinal properties (it works wonders, in my experience). There must be many others who have the same passion for rakia and the traditional methods used in its making. I know many foreigners already here who have successfully embraced rakia-culture, incorporating rakia- making into their lifestyle here. And why not? This is what happens in almost every Bulgarian household, and for good reason. Don't be fooled by the rakia you get in restaurants or supermarkets; they don't always compare to homemade rakia in the least. I have to compliment a British couple from the nearby village of General Toshevo on their own excellent rakia, sampled (well, to be honest it went well beyond the sampling stage) by me and some Bulgarian friends one weekend. He is now held in high esteem in the area, having in fact won a competition for the best rakia in the region.

SIMPLE TREASURE - 23

- A Bargain Weekend Holiday -

It was a national holiday in Bulgaria from Thursday 6th to Sunday 9th September. A four-day weekend — what could we do? My Lada car had been smashed up, so we had no transport, and with the repair bills due, no money to spare either. We deserved a holiday. The last one we had we were ill for three of the days and rushed around for guests the rest of the week. No real respite for us at all. We needed a break! What were the options with the 100 leva we had put aside for this occasion? The Black Sea coast was one, and we found that getting to Burgas only cost 4.20 leva each by train — a return journey of over 200 km for less than 4 pounds! After looking at the weather forecast we were nearly put off, with a prediction of cold and rain for the three days we had booked. All year we had sizzling temperatures and only the odd day of rain. Now on the only three days in the year we could call a holiday it was changing! However we were still very excited about sleeping for three days if the forecast came true! Quality time alone together was also was a major factor.

We scanned the Internet for cheap apartments in the coastal villages and found quite a few that were only charging 8 leva a night each. We could spend three nights for 48 leva, all with en suite bathroom, TV and sea view balcony! This particular village was some 25 km from Burgas, and we guessed the fare would be around 3 leva each for a bus to the apartment location. The total sum for travel and board was 62.40 leva. All went according to plan, apart from sharing a taxi with another couple from Burgas railway station to the village — another few leva saved.

We arrived at the apartment that we had booked on the Internet only to find ourselves being shown two other apartments in other houses in the street. We declined these and were shown the actual apartment booked but it was only 100 metres from the main coastal road. A lovely, well laid-out modern apartment with air conditioning, but the noise from the road, even with the double-glazing closed, was too much. We left and went back to the bus stop to seek alternative accommodation from apartment owners who were looking for clients getting off the buses. After a couple of inquiries we found an owner who had what we wanted, and still for only 8 leva per person per night.

The owner led us to the house, talking all the way about how expensive it was for Bulgarians to holiday nowadays and how the foreign tourists had pushed up property prices and rents in this village over the last few years. The room was on the third floor of a converted house, and had an en suite bathroom and TV but no air conditioning, though this wasn't so important to us. The room was immaculate, with snow white sheets on the comfortable beds and a balcony with a sea view and a table for evening meals and drinks. What more could we ask for, at 16 leva a night for both of us? There was also a fridge in the corridor. We had access to the quaint village centre, and to walk through to the lovely sandy beach was only a five-minute walk. This location had everything you could ask for in a resort, including some lovely restaurants and evening entertainment.

The weather was indeed cold, and the rains came, keeping us off the beach and out of the sea. Apart from a little stroll around, and the second evening going to a restaurant and then getting lost and soaked in the pouring rain tying to find our apartment, the time was spent in bed sleeping or dozing. Then a phone call from a friend changed the last twenty four hours we spent there, and we were certainly glad of the sleep we had up to that point! Another story for another time... The next day, we got a lift back to Yambol from our friend and donated 10 leva towards petrol, saving even more on the fare back. The whole four days and three nights including travel, food, drink, entertainment and even a little souvenir to take back, cost less than the 100 leva for both of us. Even on a Bulgarian wage a good price to pay for a long weekend on the coast! Without Bulgarian knowledge foreigners here would find it quite difficult to copy the cheap system we used, the Bulgarian language is the main obstacle and the fact that most people we had to deal with didn't know I was English — I have learned to keep my mouth shut at critical moments, usually when deals are done with apartment owners, shop owners and taxi drivers. Was this a Bulgarian weekend holiday at Bulgarian prices? Yes, most definitely, but we are lucky to have disposable income for this; many other Bulgarians don't. We are indeed fortunate people here in Bulgaria.

SIMPLE TREASURE - 24

- Shkembe Chorba – An Early Intro -

I first sampled Shkembe Chorba (Bulgarian Tripe Soup) a while ago in Yambol at 2:00 in the morning. This was after a very busy evening with Bulgarian friends, eating, drinking and dancing followed by more drinking, dancing and talking in a local nightclub. Just as I thought the nightclub scene was over and it was time to go home, we zigzagged our way to a non-stop bar and were presented with another round of beers, and in addition a round of tripe soup! At the time it was a real mystery as to why tripe soup was ordered, until it was explained that this soup was a perfect remedy for heavy heads after drinking sessions, usually drunk the morning after the night before! Tripe soup went out of fashion decades ago in the UK, and after this session all I can say is they just don't know what they are missing over there now. For me this was the resurrection of a dish that I thought had disappeared off the face of the earth. How could I ever doubt that the Bulgarians would continue to surprise me with their taste and food fashions?

Shkembe Chorba was enjoyed to the hilt, with fresh bread (there was an all-night bakery open round the corner from the bar) and garnished with dried, roughly-ground chilli peppers, garlic, vinegar and salt. Such a simple dish touches taste buds on all corners of the tongue, resulting in a clearer head and constitution to walk home with. I may also add that at no time does the descriptive word 'drunk' portray an evening like this. Bulgarians generally do not get drunk — just merrier, as the evening turns into morning. Bulgarian company, food, talk and dance help enormously. Shkembe Chorba is mainly chopped up calf stomach lining, cooked in a milk-based liquid with garlic, vinegar and chilli peppers as seasoning.

Shkembe Chorba Recipe:

If you drink, you must learn how to make Shkembe Chorba, the Bulgarian cure for alcoholic indulgence. This recipe has been in my Bulgarian partner Galia's family for generations and is no longer a secret.

Ingredients:

1/2 kg tripe (calf belly)
120 ml sunflower oil
250 ml fresh milk
1 tsp paprika
black pepper (freshly ground)
salt
garlic (peeled and roughly sliced)
red wine vinegar
hot chilli (dried and roughly ground with seeds)

Preparation: Boil the tripe for a couple of minutes then clean both sides of the tripe with a knife until it is completely free of marks and film. Rinse well, place in a pot of cold water and bring to the boil. Leave to simmer for around five hours, topping up the water occasionally so the tripe is submerged at all times. Remove the cooked tripe (keep the stock to one side) then cut into small chunks (some prefer it minced). Add some salt to the stock, along with the paprika, milk and oil, and boil for a further 15 minutes. Finally, add the tripe to the soup mixture and it's ready to serve. Serve in soup bowls or deep dishes, along with salt, vinegar, chopped garlic and more roughly-ground hot chilli served alongside. A basket of fresh bread to accompany is also customary.

Notes: This dish should not be served with any alcoholic beverage as it's the Bulgarian cure for a hangover. However, you might want to go on another binge just for an excuse to try this again afterwards.

SIMPLE TREASURE - 25

- Bulgarian Tundzha Fish -

Bulgaria never fails to amaze me in every aspect, and today was no exception in the town of Yambol, my Monday-to-Friday home. Yambol straddles the river Tundzha, which is not only beautiful as it meanders through the town but also has its practical uses, one of which I was about to discover that evening. A hard day at work had finished and I had a pleasant walk home in the warm September sunshine. I build up a good hunger every day at this time, and find that dinner is always in progress in the kitchen on my arrival just before 6:00. Well, this is to be expected from Galia and her Baba Mama, who through tradition have found it their duty to prepare food for the working men of the house.

Galia's son and I turn up at about the same time each evening and today was no exception. As I entered the house there was something different this evening, the aroma of fresh fish was in the air and my mouth was watering already. Galia's brother had brought home some fish that he and his brother had caught from the Tundzha River earlier in the day. I could see that they had already been gutted and were minus their heads; lucky old Alex, another Bulgarian doorbell dog, would get these for his evening meal, much to his delight! They were preparing the fish very simply, dipping them in flour and frying them in a shallow pan of sunflower oil. A taste you would pay a hefty sum for in the UK. Before long we had a plateful of Tundzha fish ready to eat; but where were the chips? This is a natural reaction to any Brit upon seeing fish on the menu. The answer was no chips, but beer. Somehow fish and beer had this chalk and cheese feeling about it, but I changed my mind about this a few moments later.

We sat down to the fish and a glass of cold Shumensko beer, with soft, fresh Yambol-baked bread and raw garlic; another Bulgarian taste of heaven. The bones took a little negotiating, but after a little while I got the technique, and the meat just fell away from the bone. This left sweet, succulent meat that just melted in the mouth. Each mouthful of fish was followed by a bite of the raw garlic and a piece of bread, and washed down each time — after a 'Nazdrave!' — with a sip of beer. It was like a synchronised fish-eating contest. Adding to the enjoyment of this healthy feast was the fact that it only cost a few leva, for the beer and bread. This is how it is in Bulgaria; making the most of natural resources.

SIMPLE TREASURE - 26

- Bulgarian Tundzha Fishing -

So I had eaten fish from the Tundzha, and that was a wonderful event. It was now time for me to turn hunter and provide for the family, but this was no chore; I love fishing, but never seem to have the time for it! This was a family affair, as Galia's two sons teamed up with me to form a team of fish hunters prowling the Tundzha, and their experience in fishing here, finding the right spots, using the right tackle and bait, was the key to success. We all travelled by bicycle, very much in the tradition for most Bulgarian coarse fishermen here. In fact a car would have trouble getting to the spot that we found, even with the dry state of the Tundzha's banks. I won't divulge the location of the exact spot that we found in this publication, for fear of it being over-fished by others. The bait was Bulgarian worms, and no sooner had we cast than the first fish was taken. The river is quite fast-flowing, but where we were there was a pool of relatively still water in a small bay, so the fishing was quite easy, without the need to recast every minute. The scenery here was outstanding: the countryside spread out in front of us and the dominant white blocks of Yambol town standing tall behind us.

After about an hour we had at least twenty fish, enough for a meal and a half, and we began to pack our kit away. We threw back many that were too small — and of course the big carp that got away at one point in the session — yes, really! As we made our way home, further up the bank we saw a couple of Roma fishing with homemade contraptions. I wanted to know how they set this up, and asked to see their equipment close-up. They of course obliged, while Galia's two sons looked on, amazed at the fact that I wanted to know. What I discovered was fascinating. The rod was a bamboo cane; there was no reel, just some old string tied to the end of the cane. I wondered how on earth they could catch fish using just string as the line.

This mystery was soon solved as they pulled the tackle out of the water. At the end of the string was tied about a metre of fishing line and the rest of the tackle was attached to this: a float that was actually a small, dried pepper that had been painted to make it waterproof, and the weights used to make this sit upright in the water, small metal buttons. The hook was the only commercial part of the kit, with some sweetcorn as bait. Even more fascinating than this was that they had caught bigger fish we had! This was another truly amazing discovery of how things can be done here on the cheap, and as we went back to hand over the fish to the women cooks, I just couldn't forget what I saw; I just love this country, the people and its ways!

SIMPLE TREASURE - 27

- Bulgarian Bikes and Roma Riders -

Bulgarians and bikes — the push/pedal bike kind that is! What a variety there is, but ninety-nine per cent are the cheapest kind, because Bulgarians just can't afford designer machines. For that reason top of the range bikes are not available in the country, as there is no demand. To a Bulgarian, if a bike works and does the job and is cheap, or even costs nothing, then that's the option they will take. There are those who do have cycling as a hobby, a serious hobby in some cases; I know one particular man who is a fanatical cyclist, with the top bikes and all the gear. I see him out on the Yambol highways sometimes, but he is an exception to the rule. Most cyclists here ride boneshakers, and the variety of homemade bikes is fantastic, it's almost like watching clowns riding circus bikes.

The most entertaining variety of bikes are those ridden by the Roma riders. One evening while I was walking home I heard a screeching clatter of metal, the kind of sound that makes you want to cringe. Turning round, I saw a Roma on a bike, the compulsory plastic box strapped to the carrier with old string, this time filled with cardboard, moving very slowly along the roughly cobbled road. The cause of the clattering was due to the front wheel of the bike lacking a tyre — he was riding on the bare metal rim. I stopped in my tracks and stared as this Roma rider slowly clattered past me. At the same time he was staring back at me, as if to say, 'What's the problem?' Mind you, there was still a continuous smile behind that questioning look as he rode off into the distance.

There are more shows that go on in the Bulgarian Biking World that have to be seen to be believed: balancing acts, one bike ridden by the whole family, trailers, dog-powered bikes, even a one-wheeled bike with skateboard wheels fixed to the front forks. Many bikes aren't actually ridden, but used as baggage carriers, and by golly can they carry a lot. Most bikes (apart from the new ones) don't have brakes either; they rely on the Fred Flintstone method — smoking feet!

SIMPLE TREASURE - 28

- Yambol Fashion -

Bulgarian fashion is stylish to say the least. You cannot fail to be impressed by the variety of chic clothing that is worn by the beautiful women and so effectively modelled in the towns and cities here. The perfect complement to beautiful Yambol: women and fashion. How lucky can you get, being a man here? Today something struck me as very funny, but by no means unique, is how fashion can be taken at face value here. It was just a glimpse out of the office window this morning; there before me was a sight that made me laugh so much tears rolled down my cheeks. A very large middle-aged mother was waddling down the down the hill towards Yambol bus station. She was dressed in a lovely oversized brown blouse, which is the norm for many women that possess such a figure. Nothing strange about that, I hear you say. As the blouse was flapping about in the warm Yambol breeze, I noticed some English text on the front it — something that I doubt any self-respecting middle-aged overweight Bulgarian mother would have chosen, and that I hope was chosen in complete obliviousness of the meaning. It read:

SEX INSTRUCTOR — FIRST LESSON FREE

Needless to say I don't think she'll get many customers! There are many Bulgarian women here that could wear that garment and there would be queues — made up of course of only English speaking clients!

SIMPLE TREASURE - 29

- Bulgarian Crime — The Attraction -

Crime in the UK is still on the climb and it is hard to imagine anyone in the UK who has not been directly or indirectly affected by this. There are many more reasons to leave the UK other than rising crime and the diminishing of a fair judicial system; however, it is still one of the main reasons for people wanting to leave Britain. It is fair to say that a good proportion of the British just put up with things as crime spirals its way out of control, affecting the quality of life, and indeed freedom, for the vast majority of people. Some of course don't even realise that other ways of life exist away from this, and still regard the UK as the centre of the universe, come rain or shine. Well, fair play to them, but a shame. I suggest looking at others who have had the vision and have tried it, giving testimonies that ring true and providing hope that attracts others who don't want to be the pioneers or risk-takers. Many follow on once a pathway has been trodden, and form expatriate communities abroad. Safety in numbers of their own kind is a comfort for many.

Back to Britain, where it seems that law-abiding people are being put through the mill of an ill society, one that fails to protect them before, during and after crime strikes. A country that has become so self-righteously moralistic, the whole system is being strangled. Crime is now firmly rooted in UK society, part of the culture, because in many cases it pays, but it goes much deeper than that. In Bulgaria crime exists, but it is dealt with in a totally different way: criminals are actually punished when caught! Sometimes injustice may seem to have been done, perhaps on occasion innocent parties are punished, but this is not common. I think these instances should be looked upon as an acceptable level of tolerance within the system. No system is perfect; you have to look at the overall effectiveness of the system in place, not just at the little nuts and bolts.

I can imagine many do-gooders building up a head of steam over this, but look again at what this shows in respect for the law, and look again at how you see things in your patch. No one has a right to judge other countries' systems of law; in fact Bulgaria has as much right to tell Britain how to run their system. Look at the overall effectiveness of the system — look at what puts people off committing crime — and then ask the question: Where exactly is the crime rate highest? In many people's books there should be a fear of doing something criminal. This just doesn't seem to be the case in the UK, but it is here in Bulgaria. The police are feared here (as opposed to being respected in many instances) and this, in conjunction with a sprinkling of corruption within, may be deemed as an acceptable situation that helps the police system work. Carefully negotiating the tightrope of law-enforcement is how it is for most Bulgarian citizens, and how it works here. And yes, Mafia do work here, doing their Mafia thing; but Mafia exist worldwide, and have deep roots embedded in the UK. They seem to be feared by all, including the police, but again this hierarchy is worldwide.

When the streets aren't safe to walk in the day, never mind the night, then there is something terribly wrong with that society. You can do this in the vast majority of areas in Bulgaria. If truth be told, you are more likely to get attacked by an inquisitive donkey than a mugger in most of the country, and that is rare enough. Worldwide, cities and large towns attract criminal activities, and Bulgaria is no exception, but that's really where it ends. Then there's the Roma. The Roma are a different story, but again we all live with them worldwide, some more comfortably than others. So Bulgaria is a destination where the crime rate is nonexistent in many areas. That is the big appeal for so many. I am lucky enough to live in one of those areas, where mine and countless other villages are a totally crime-free society. The community doesn't need police, as they know that everyone knows what is right and wrong in the local community. They police themselves!

SIMPLE TREASURE - 30

- Schools or Fashion Houses? -

Every year at the end of the summer months, the normally quiet Bulgarian streets are transformed: suddenly there are swarms of children making their way to school! This year, looking around in the morning, the children thronging the streets gave the impression that they were heading to a fashion show rather than to school. With no mandatory school uniform, the dress trends were spectacular to say the least. From where I'm standing Bulgarian fashion is in good hands with the youth of today. Colourful and interesting as it is watching the children catwalk to school, this is a big financial strain on parents who are subjected to the cry of want from their very fashion-conscious children. This pressure comes from various sources of direct and indirect advertising, aimed at this impressionable age group: Bulgaria has its law, but it's not based on moral grounds. As an example, school uniform has not been introduced to prevent discrimination against the poor who can't afford the latest fashion — it just isn't important enough to consider and never a problem. This creates a situation of the 'haves' and 'have-nots' that would be intolerable in the eyes of the modern western world, but the rich and the poor here not intolerant of each other but live harmoniously. There is never any jealousy or protest about it, it's just accepted that how things are.

Somehow, though, I don't think compulsory school uniform will come into force any time soon in Bulgaria. After all, they had fifty years of uniform-clad children pre-1990, and there's no going back now, with the taste of fashion freedom now firmly established. The Bulgarian acceptance of the divide between the rich and the poor is more or less accepted as normal now. The poor are not looked down upon by the rich and in turn do not look with a jealous eye at the rich. They may have better homes and cars, but the food is essentially the same. The gap between the rich and poor in Bulgaria is still widening, but it wasn't that long ago when equality ruled. The transformation has come about so quickly that the previous regime of socialist equality has been left behind in many Bulgarian minds.

- Bulgarian Police — How it is Here -

The job of a Bulgarian policeman has always seemed to me to be a bit of a perk job. Many Bulgarian children, when asked what they want to do when they grow up, say they want to be policemen (mainly boys of course). It is the case that the police have a lot of respect from the Bulgarian public, and they are not hidebound by a mass of rules and regulations that stop them doing their job. A short vacation with my partner found the weather unusually cold and wet, therefore beach and sea activities were restricted, and we spent the rest of the time in bed sleeping or dozing. A friend rang to say that she was seeing someone on the coast and we should meet up and party on. We agreed! Her friend was a policeman working in the Black Sea region. They turned up in the coastal village where we were staying, and some twenty minutes later the party began.

Christo, the policeman, was a man of typical Bulgarian build, short, stocky, with a beer belly, piercing blue eyes, no chin and slightly greying neatly-cut hair. His shorts showed thin-calved legs without hair; I don't think they were shaved, but his arms, shown off by his plain short-sleeved shirt were definitely not. Apart from a pair of good quality brown leather, his other accessory was his GSM — this man just didn't stop talking, and it was in constant use, planning the party for his newly acquired guests, whom he obviously wanted to impress. Like most Bulgarian men Christo treated his girlfriend with a little disdain, dominating conversations totally, giving a one-man show, but you couldn't fail to like the guy; he was a very charming and confident person. Using my limited Bulgarian we gave each other basic resumes, and I found that Christo and I liked many of the same things — essentially, Bulgarian food, drink, football and life here in general. I found out that being a policeman was a good life in Bulgaria, and that the perks are never ending: not too dissimilar from being a mafia man, without having to look over your shoulder every moment of the day!

We had just finished a beer or two in the bar, and I was asked to get provisions for the day as we were off to other towns further south. Drunk or not, and in the present company, Christo told me that beer and cars can mix here, but only in the villages, where no high speeds are reached; there's one rule, just don't crash! So were off in Christo's car — this was another new experience to behold! If you have driven in Bulgaria you may have seen those cars that flash past you regardless of oncoming traffic. Well this was one of those cars, and it certainly sobers you up, that's for sure! I found that closing my eyes was the key to a less stressful journey, as seeing the road ahead felt like playing Russian roulette. There was a police check en route, but a high-speed wave and a shout to the police on duty saw us through — they knew Christo and his car, and they waved him on.

We arrived in a town further south and stopped at a shop on the main road for cigarettes. With no parking on the crowded street, Christo simply parked in the middle of the road, blocking the traffic behind. A man started complaining outside the shop, until Christo got out of the car and he shut up when he recognised him as the law. The honks from the cars behind soon stopped too, as Christo was recognised and the word went round. Everyone deferred to the law here: he seemed to know everyone in the town, chatting with everyone that passed while carrying on a constant conversation via GSM. Cigarettes were duly bought for the women. Christo and I don't smoke: Christo remarked that you could die a slow and painful death from smoking. I agreed, but then I thought if he preferred a quick and painless death that might explain his driving style.

Finally we un-blocked the road simply by driving off heading towards the coast with Christo receiving a farewell chorus of 'Ciao!' from shop-owners on both sides of the street. This time our destination was pin pointed to a restaurant on the coast, in a superb setting one could only dream of. The preferential treatment continued: we were shown a prime a table and served before others who had turned up earlier, all due to Christo's status and the respect shown to him here. A meal of freshly cooked fish arrived, along with more beer. We weren't allowed to pay — as Christo approached the cashier at the bar, all I saw exchanged was conversation! Then it was off to a newly-built hotel with its own bar and swimming pool, and free drinks all round at the owner's insistence. During this time we were told that we could have free apartments booked in another coastal resort. We moved off again, racing at Formula One speed further down the coastal road, still with the GSM in full use, Christo making more plans as we travelled.

A little while later we pulled up at a fantastically luxurious hotel and were shown around by the owner, then escorted to our room for the night. This was all a complimentary offering from the owner to his policeman friend Christo. Still everyone bowed to his presence: some locally-caught fresh fish were brought along and offered to us but we just didn't have the facility to keep them overnight, and declined. These were big healthy carp, caught from local inland waters, which I found strange in a place just fifty metres from the Black Sea. It just so happened that the Bulgarian national football team was playing in the European Cup qualifying matches this particular evening, so the TV was booked exclusively for Christo and his guests. Not only that, food and rakia were to be laid on for the evening: more complimentary gifts from the hotel manager!

We freshened up and spent a few hours watching the football, downing two bottles of grape rakia along with various traditional foods. Non-stop talking was the main activity, and was quite distracting for me as I tried to watch the game. It was interesting getting feedback from Christo when the opposition scored. I had to actually tell him they had scored before he replied with a resigned 'Normal'; this was a typical Bulgarian reaction. The same 'Normal' was made in response to the final score of 2-0. Christo had for many years accepted that most European sides were better than Bulgaria, but I was taken back a bit by his lack of emotion during the ups and downs of the match. Talking occupied the evening, and enthusiasm for football was well down the league of interest, well below rakia and food. Perhaps the taste of defeat was inbuilt in Bulgarians and they have learned not to get too worked up about it. He accepted the defeat of his team with total resignation even before the match — this was going to happen anyway, so what was the problem?

So much for the football, the next thing we knew there was a Mercedes and driver waiting outside to pick us up and whisk us to a discotheque in a neighbouring town. Moments later and all feeling like Cinderella going to a ball, we entered the lively discotheque. What a fantastic venue! It was state of the art, all mod cons and all done on a massive scale. The entry fee was waived, as was the cost of all the drink that was served to us throughout the rest of the evening. Christo was the host of the venue along with his three guests; in effect he was the VIP this evening, and we tagged along. We danced the night away and then had another chauffeur-driven Mercedes to drive us back to the hotel, but not before having a little party with some traffic police on duty in the town; again, time doesn't matter here. You go to bed when you are tired, and by 4:30 am we were!

The next morning breakfast was taken at a beach restaurant only a hundred metres away from the hotel, with no lapse in VIP treatment, as they were expecting us. No doubt Christo's GSM had been in action again to prepare this earlier. We filled up with a Bulgarian pancake breakfast and more beer, and it was getting on to midday as we soaked up the final moments on the other side of the Bulgarian coin. Finally a trip back to our village apartment and Christo went on his own way back to work. He was still on his GSM as we waved goodbye, watching him drive off into the mysterious world of deciding what is right and wrong in Bulgarian daily life. Two years ago it would have been difficult, nigh on impossible, to come to terms with situations such as this, but you learn here how to take things as they come and not try and fight against everything. I wouldn't have enjoyed this before, but learning how to enjoy yourself and not feel totally indebted to these people, with their unbounded generosity and kindness, comes with time.

It was a whirlwind twenty-four hours, and a view of how the other half live in Bulgaria: from poverty-stricken communities trying to make ends meet and to the perspective of an individual in the community that finds the good things in life come their way through job status and respect. All the time I was thinking 'What had Christo done beyond this role as a community policeman to get such treatment?' The only thing I could come up with was that he might turn a blind eye to certain things that go on — I might be wrong, but that's how it felt. As for the Bulgarian police, well, they are only human; perhaps too human in view of what I experienced, but the respect remains for the law as administered by the police, which works for the main part. It really is a case of hands-on policing, with the community as part of the policing system. Community policing technically up and running effectively, well before it was re-invented and failed in the UK.

SIMPLE TREASURE - 32

- New Bulgarian Cowboys -

I found myself heading towards the village Byal Kladenets (meaning White Well) early last Saturday morning, a village situated right next to the massive reservoir that supplies the whole region electricity. My brother had a scooter, and the shortcut from Skalitsa to Byal Kladenets, cutting 10 km of the journey, was along a ploughed-up dirt track that ran past the sunflower and sweetcorn fields between the villages, filled with failed crops this year. We had to pick up two horses and transport them back to Skalitsa, as I was to look after and tend for them for a few weeks. As we made our way, both crammed onto the small scooter, there was a degree of apprehension about the journey there, and even more about the journey back. My brother has a fear of horses, and I only really have experience with a donkey and cart, not these massive, well-muscled animals. There had been a heavy rain a few days before, and as we left the road and joined the track the slipping and sliding started; in many parts we had to get off and walk our way through. This was a real problem for us, and after only a short while we wished we'd done it another day when the track had dried out; but we were now committed and had to carry on.

A sigh of relief was breathed as we finally got to the village and paused a while before going to get the two horses that were grazing on the side of the hill. Genna and Sparky, (the horses names) were being looked after by a Bulgarian neighbour, who was called to help kit them out for the cart that was waiting. This was the next problem: Genna somehow jolted away from the Bulgarian that was helping and ran free.

The next two hours were spent trying to catch her as she played games with us. Chasing her didn't work, and our minds were working overtime as our bodies rested. A lasso was the only answer, so one was made up from the tethering rope. The plan was to get Sparky out into the fields again, as Genna usually grazes next to him. Then if we got within a couple of metres of her we'd lasso her, and the job would be done.

So we did exactly that, with the Bulgarian neighbour thinking that we were crazy as he just sat on his own cart and watched from a distance. We put the plan into action, and it worked like a dream: Sparky was made the bait, and as Genna approached it was only a matter of a well-judged throw of the lasso and the job was done. The Bulgarian neighbour watched with disbelief as the new cowboy maestros strode proudly past him with the two horses. We kitted the horses up, Genna to pull the cart and Sparky to follow tied up behind, then we were off down the track that had almost completely dried up in the now blazing-hot sun. The return journey, bumping over the undulating terrain, was hard going, and it was a very tired horse that arrived in Skalitsa; we were all tired, but home and dry.

SIMPLE TREASURE - 33

- Cobblestone Yambol -

Over the past few months in Yambol there has been a great deal of repair of the roads leading in and out of the town. The main reason for this is the growth of the tree roots that spread themselves like giant underground moles, creating endless concrete waves not only on the pavements but also on the traffic-bearing roads. The Bulgarian way of fixing this is by hand; there are no massive tarmac machines to finish the job in a couple of hours. The hands-on job takes weeks, but there's a good reason for that: every road is being reconstructed with cobblestones. I really thought that the days of this type of road were coming to an end, but apparently it's still thriving in Yambol. On a bed of compacted sand each individual traditional cobblestone is placed and then sealed, giving the arching patterns so characteristic of this form of road. Whilst the road is closed for the repair and re-laying there is absolute mayhem, but the beeping of horns, the shouting of drivers trying to negotiate their way round all the road-works is very funny from a pedestrian's point of view. But then the pedestrians' plight isn't really given much consideration either, as the pavement is totally blocked with piles of stone and sand, and to walk these streets means either being running the gauntlet of the traffic or high-jumping over the bright yellow safety tape. Prams and pushchairs have to contend with an assault course more suited to an army training exercise. Do they complain? No, not an ounce as they make their way un-flustered through the obstacles set in front of them. I suppose it has always been this way, and the residents of Yambol are well versed in dealing with this. It's a small price to pay, considering how unattractive a lot of modern development can be, for Yambol to remain a lovely cobbled town in many places. Well worth the inconvenience.

SIMPLE TREASURE - 34

- Bulgarian Birthday Party -

Galia and I had been invited to the birthday party of one of her friends who lives just a five minute walk from our house in Yambol. I had been told that her husband was a hotel chef and that the food was to be scrumptious and in plentiful supply, with homemade rakia to accompany it. I'd had a bad day and to be honest I didn't really want to go, but we had promised and Galia said that a few rakia in the evening would be good after such a terrible day. We took the simple gift of a jersey and a single flower, along with a chocolate bar for their 3-year-old son, and set off along the cobblestone streets towards the house. This young Bulgarian family live right next to a Roma neighbourhood, and we could hear the music of a Roma band as we got closer.

It got louder and louder and when we turned into their street there was a Roma street party in full swing, and it was only 6:30 in the evening. This is a daily happening in Yambol in this area and can be heard far and wide. No one complained, as the pulsating, heaving beat of the chalga was a privilege to have around — and free! I can imagine many foreigners looking at the same situation and pulling their hair out. This is what happens here, and now I really can see the sense in enjoying the situation rather than getting frustrated and stressed out with what before I would have described as an invasion of unwanted sound in 'my space!' We approached the front door — a better term might be barricade — a thick metal red-painted façade, with no discernible features. Well, this was Roma territory; perhaps even letterboxes would present a possible breach of security here. From an outsider's point of view this was a dump of an area, and the birthday house was on the side of a litter-covered road in a state of total disrepair; it looked like a field ploughed up for winter.

Somehow I knew that inside the house would be a complete contrast to the chaos outside, just like the apartments in the tower blocks — simply, beautifully-kept and very clean Bulgarian havens. I wasn't disappointed. We took off our shoes to walk on the pristine carpets and ceramic tiled floors that you really felt the urge to skate on. The iron door slowly swung shut, and the open-air Roma concert gradually segued into Bulgarian folk-pop music playing somewhere in the house. Katia, the hostess and Bulgarian birthday girl, was given birthday greetings and was wished good health, good luck, good business and luck in love, which is a traditional greeting after the initial birthday compliments. The gifts were gratefully received and the formalities were over. The inside of the house was completely modern, spotless with plain white walls and ceiling. As we were led into the living area a table with food fit for a king was laid both meticulously and symmetrically. The snow-capped shopska salad mountains stole the limelight from the myriad other delights, still in their virgin state! Another Bulgarian couple turned up half and hour later; more friends, more talking, more food and drink and the party began to swing. As always the women worked around the men, who only moved to have their pictures taken or change the music, and the latter only because the women were in the kitchen preparing more food. Well, that isn't entirely true: the husband, as I said, was a chef; furthermore, he had prepared all the food before we arrived. This is very rare, so I am told, and from what I see on a daily basis I entirely believe it.

It was now approaching midnight, the first occasion that the time was remarked upon; time is not so important here, it is how you feel that counts, and we were all full of the food and drink that just kept on flowing: rakia with the salad and beer with the meat course, a beautiful, melt-in-the-mouth pork with mushrooms and a sauce moat around a rice castle. The dessert was no less special: home-baked sponge cake (they save the candles from birthday cakes to use during power-cuts). This was moist and delicious, with a middling sweetness, enough to satisfy these sweet-toothed Bulgarians but not too overpowering for me. All washed down with lemonade. I said it was food fit for a king — midnight had struck, but the only thing that had turned into a pumpkin was my stomach! The characteristic elements of a Bulgarian birthday party are the same for any gathering of Bulgarian friends and family — food, drink, music and not least talk. We left in the early hours of the morning, when even the Roma party in the Yambol streets had run out of energy. It was only then, in the dead quiet of the night, with an almost full moon showing us the way home, that time suddenly seemed important, with the spectre of work the next morning. But in true Bulgarian fashion we didn't rush home.

- Ugly Bulgarian Baby - Not! -

In Skalitsa one of my lovely neighbours recently had a baby — I had not seen the new addition to Skalitsa village for a month or so and found it quite strange, in fact quite worrying. It was a girl, called Alexandra, and that's all the information that the family would give out. On asking around about why the baby was being hidden from the public, I discovered that it was a tradition that families with new arrivals were not to get visits from friends and family for up to a couple months after birth, as this was deemed as bad luck. This explained a lot.

Then on a lovely summer day, I saw the pram being pushed down the road past my house, and as Galia and I were also on the road walking the other way we paused to finally get a glimpse of the child. Now my Bulgarian isn't excellent by any account, but I distinctly heard Galia say in Bulgarian that the baby wasn't very pretty, added to which she said that the left eye was bigger than the right one! I was absolutely certain that this is what she said. Also, uncharacteristically, we only spent about a minute with Alexandra and Maria, his mother; usually a conversation would last anything up to an hour, especially after not seeing them for so long! When we walked away I questioned Galia, who said that it wasn't good to spend time looking at the baby, it was a bad thing to do in Bulgaria. I then asked why she insulted the baby by saying it was ugly and remarking on its eyes. She said this was a custom in Bulgaria — you say bad things about the baby, as it brings good luck. I was quite amazed and also amused by this.

The following weekend we met up again with baby Alexandra and mother Maria, and I had the experience of following this strange custom by telling the mother in Bulgarian that her son had ears like Prince Charles and a mouth like a horse. She thanked me very much as she strolled off to her next brief encounter!

SIMPLE TREASURE - 36

- Ground and Cooled Coffee -

Everyday I see groups of big hefty Roma women wandering the streets of Yambol. Not what you think, as they wear bright orange fluorescent jackets, and are armed with a couple of traffic cones and a broom. They look like Roma witches as they make their way to work. Have you guessed their profession yet? Cleaning the streets, and by Jove do they do a good job. If it wasn't for the Bulgarian habit of dropping litter wherever they want they would be out of a job. They appear before 7:30, as I usually walk alongside them from the Roma quarters in the north part of the town towards the town centre. They have a mustering point that resembles a Steptoe and Son junkyard, with a corrugated iron fence surround and some well-worn steps they sit on. The steps are used as a seating place for their lunchtime break, a long five and a half hours later. As I walk home for lunch I see them swigging bottles of beer, with used plastic bags on their laps as plates.

As always the Roma are even louder than the Bulgarians; it seems as if they are arguing all the time, but that's not the case — they're just talking in their own way. When they work in the streets of Yambol they are non-stop, picking up every trace of litter then sweeping the dust, not a speck left behind, as if their lives depended on it. Watching them work you would think their pay was on commission or they faced a deduction from their wage if any rubbish remained. I actually dare not think how little they get in the first place, but I know that the minimum wage here is 180 leva per month (around 15 pounds a week). This morning as usual I was following a group of four of these brightly clad Roma workers (why they are all obese is beyond me, with the amount of walking they do everyday). One was sipping black coffee out of a small plastic vending machine cup. She took down the final sip and flung the clear plastic cup into the road! Now although this was true Bulgarian style, coming from a street cleaner it was in fact quite bizarre. I supposed she would clean it up later that day! For a fleeting moment I just didn't understand this but then I did — it makes complete sense. This is the Bulgarian Roma ensuring there is always going to be work for them, essentially an action of job creation.

The coffee stories continue with a coffee shop that opens very early in the morning where Bulgarian Roma workers pop in to get takeaway coffee. Every day I see people buying coffee and either sitting down in the seating area on the pavement waiting for the coffee to cool down before drinking it or just walking away with it. Today there was a slightly different slant with one customer whom I saw buying a coffee. He arrived on a typical loud and smoky moped with a helmet that seemed to have been knitted by his Baba Mama. Most people light a cigarette with their coffee and that's their breakfast, this thin and ghostly figure did just that but in the cafe whilst the coffee was being ordered. He held the coffee in one bare hand and wore a glove on the other hand. With his cigarette held by his thin lips and tilted downward he made his way to his moped. Now the coffee was too hot to drink so what was he going to do? He said good morning to me and I returned the compliment and asked if the coffee was indeed hot - small talk and talking about the obvious is common with Bulgarians. He confirmed it was hot and then wished me a goodbye as he started up his moped again. The next thing I knew, he was riding the bike into the distance, after a negotiated bounce from the pavement into the road with one hand, and the other holding both the hot coffee and cigarette as he made his way to work. What a good idea for cooling coffee, should be cool enough to drink after a kilometre or two!

SIMPLE TREASURE - 37

- Bad Brits in Bulgaria -

Two UK nationals were given eight-month suspended sentences and three years to be served on probation for attacking policemen in Bulgaria's town of Veliko Tarnovo recently. On a daily basis, en route to a home-cooked lunch, I always pass the police station in Yambol. This is also the place where Bulgarians and foreigners get their resident permits and Lichna Carta. This being the case you occasionally hear English being spoken as folk make their way there from the town centre or hang around the area at lunchtime while it is closed. On this I day I picked up the distinct English accents of a family making their way up the hill toward the police station. I tend to keep my mouth shut on these occasions, as the lunch waiting on the table at home would get cold if I delayed. And on this instance I was very glad I did. Bulgarian parking systems on the pavements in Yambol meant that I was forced to follow behind the English-speaking group in single file whilst walking up the hill. This gave me an opportunity to overhear a conversation that on reflection I wish I'd never heard.

It was about getting rat-arsed on the previous Saturday night at a stag night on the Black Sea coast. They went on, talking about smashing a window, trashing the hotel room they were staying in and roughing up the hotel manager who had 'the cheek' to complain in the morning. They spoke with pride in their voices, as laughter followed each description of event. In the process their limited vocabulary was mixed with a limited variety of abusive adjectives. To add to this one of the foreigners was pushing a pram with a child in it — what a future for that child! Now this was something that embarrassed the living daylights out of me. I just hoped and prayed that they weren't applying for Bulgarian resident permits as they turned off toward the entrance of the police station. They should really have been going there to face charges!

Most things that go on in Yambol are pleasant experiences but on occasion something shakes you up a bit. This was just such an instance, although it had nothing to do with Bulgaria or the Bulgarians, but undesirable outsiders who feel they have license to do what they want without fear of punishment. So when the media report a case where punishment is given for this type of behaviour it is actually good news. But what did they get? In the Veliko Tarnovo case the result was a suspended sentence. What is that in terms of punishment? Well, nothing really. Perhaps this sentence would not have been handed out to Bulgarians in the same situation.

Fortunately this type of behaviour is very rare in Yambol and its surrounds, and this was the only instance in all the time I have lived and worked here in Yambol. Whatever the future holds, with more of these people coming to Bulgaria, the attraction of this region remains for decent law-abiding foreigners with a respect for how things are here. Some Black Sea resorts however will always bring in summer madness from foreigners, which is why I am so glad I live away from all that.

SIMPLE TREASURE - 38

- Well-Behaved Bees -

Bees are very different over here, as I found when it was time to harvest the grapes from the garden. The grapes, after the weather and starlings had had their share, were to be gathered and turned into the wine and, the most renowned tradition of Bulgaria, the rakia. Quite a fear came over me as I approached the grapes, based on my previous experiences of bees and wasps two thousand miles away. Many a brave soul would run from British bees and wasps; they always seemed to have an attitude problem, something that I remembered every time I saw one in Bulgaria up to this point. The humming of the bees became quite deafening to the ear as I tackled the hanging grapes. It was clear that part of the harvest was currently being shared by yet another winged species of thieves.

The bees initially pierce the skin of the grape to make their way to the sweet grape juice within, after which they buzz back to their hives and deposit the sweet content, which then turns up in jars in the Yambol market a few weeks later. I should have a stake in this honey made from my grapes, as a good tenth of the crop had been poached by the bees for someone else to profit on. So a fear of getting hurt by these bees was a consideration that I was forced to subject myself to. I could wait until dusk, when the bees go back to their hives to sleep, but then it gets dark very quickly, and since this job would take a couple of hours that wasn't really an option. It had to be done now; there would be no time early in the morning either.

Gingerly I put my hand into bunches of grapes, its interior full of feasting bees. The buzzing became more intense the further I pushed my hand into the crop. After a few disturbances I found that the bees would realise that there was something going on, and they would just drop off and fly away. They never became aggressive; even if I accidentally touched one when reaching up they would still not turn against me. It got to the stage where gently tapping the stem from which the grapes hung prior to cutting them would clear that area of bees. It was a warning that the party was over and their feast was now at an end. If I could speak bee I would swear they were thanking me and saying 'Goodbye, see you next year.' Two hours of grape harvesting in not quite reaching swarm status but quite close to it in stages and not once did any bee act aggressively, and I wasn't stung were once. What a nice kind bunch of bees Bulgaria has and what a difference from the nasty aggressive little beasts I had endured growing up in the UK. Now, with the grape harvest in, for the first time in nearly forty years I've learned about the birds and the bees all over again; this time without embarrassment or blushes.

SIMPLE TREASURE - 39

- Bulgarian Trees -

Trees in Bulgaria are the pillars of the land, accorded enormous respect by Bulgarians from all walks of life, from village to Central Government — a refreshing change in this world of waste and selfish profit-making. The tree has a wealth of uses to the Bulgarian, and a replanting policy throughout the country will ensure that the tree-covered area will remain at around thirty per cent.

Where do we start with the uses of the tree? The warmth from the fire, giving heat in the winter and cooking at all times. Trees bear fruit, nuts, berries, leaves for brewing tea and various other goodies — not only for human consumption but also for animal feed — and are a renewable source each year. The fallen leaves provide more feed and fertility for the ground they rot on. Wood is the staple material of the Bulgarian home and its surroundings, from fencing to brooms, from toothpicks to rockets and from rabbit traps to car-jacks. Trees are used for hanging goats and sheep when skinning them, and shaved twigs are used to clean out the intestines. And of course they are even used as swings by children. The list goes on — most handmade items are made from wood; carts pulled by horse and donkey are largely wooden, and even the chassis on this popular means of working transport is usually still made from wood.

Dead wood is a natural waste product, collected and used by Bulgarians for burning; this collection of dead wood for heating is legal and is common practice throughout the year. Trees provide shady areas for all that need it in the hot summer climate: a cooler area for crops to grow; shelter for humans and animals, and a haven for birds and insects alike. Where would Bulgarian dogs go without a Bulgarian tree? Bulgarian men use them for leaning on to talk, and for stubbing out the accompanying cigarette; for falling asleep under; for giving the odd kick when in a bad mood; and to hide from the wife after a few rakias.... These are just a few of the uses I have personally seen in my village. The list really is endless. On a more serious note the tree and the wood from it is what much of Bulgaria is made from: it is still is a wood culture, with housing made from wooden structures, and even wooden scaffolding and supports used for the concrete walls and ceilings in new apartment blocks. And where would the Bulgarians be without their beloved sliva tree?

SIMPLE TREASURE - 40

- Gardens and Maintenance -

If you have property in Bulgaria land management can be easy, if organised with the help of the friendly Bulgarian community, and it can make your visits here so much more enjoyable. A big concern for many is the maintenance of grounds whilst away from their property. What makes it worse is that many visitors have taken on big areas of land, not really taking into account that these will need maintenance. These are Bulgarian gardens, and the growth rate of weeds and grasses is extraordinary, especially between April and August. Unless there is someone maintaining your garden, on a weekly basis or even a daily basis, in the spring, the work can rapidly become overwhelming. This area of garden maintenance is another topic in itself — there are no short cuts in terms of the attention that gardens require. The management of waste ground or fields that you may have alongside your property can be a big help. To the livestock holder this is a haven of hay, and food that is needed for storing through the winter.

Often the question is raised as to how much to pay a local to cut the hay on occasions, just to keep it down. Well this shouldn't be a question: in most cases the feed alone should pay for the effort. If the local didn't cut his hay there he would be cutting it elsewhere for nothing after all. This is what my neighbour does on my vacant field; all the feed he gets is payment enough. (Well, on occasion he gets a rakia thrown in, but he gets that anyway!) Perhaps the ground is not suitable for hay or it is of such poor quality it isn't worth cutting for animal feed. If this is the case, and you have access to a tractor, then twice a year the land can be ploughed over, in November and February. Everyone in your neighbourhood will know someone who has a tractor; your local mayor will certainly know someone. Ploughing can be arranged locally beforehand or during November and February, when tractors are out and about ploughing other land. All land should already have access points for tractors: it would be very unusual if it didn't. You will also have to ensure that keys for locks on the gates are left with neighbours. November is the best time to plough, just before the winter frosts set in. The soil will then break down over the winter, giving fine topsoil in the spring when it's ploughed again in February. At the time you are over here in Bulgaria, try to get this organised with your locals, it's not difficult, but don't give in to being ripped off — better to leave it than pay over the odds. It is difficult to come over for your holidays and have an overgrown field on your doorstep; many spend the first few days getting it hacked down. The secret is to make provisions for this beforehand so you don't have to spend half your holiday behind a lawnmower.

SIMPLE TREASURE - 41

- 'New' Fire Engines in Yambol? -

Every day I walk past the fire station in Yambol there's always something happening. There's a great comradeship among the firemen who work there, and they have had a very busy time this year, with forest fires all around the area. Of course they also have a lot of time to kill, and on most occasions they are seen hanging around in groups talking, or working under the bonnet of a colleague's car, usually an old Lada that needs servicing. Before today I had never spoken to any of them, apart from a polite good morning or a good day, as everyone does when you pass people here. We were walking towards the town centre, and Galia had stopped for the third time to speak to another friend. It's very hard to get from A to B with Galia, who has friends everywhere. This one worked in the lottery office, well, more of a furnished trailer than an office, actually. She was in the street, away from the cash desk, talking with her brother, who was a fireman; while the women chatted, I spoke to the brother.

His most striking feature was his proud grey moustache, which perfectly matched his grey fireman's uniform, with its old-style brass fireman's helmet badge high up on the sleeve of the jacket. He was a well-built man, as all the firemen are, with hands the Hulk would be proud of. He was astride a very old Simpson moped. I could see the cracks in the tyre tread from age, and a multi-coloured head scarf tied round the headlamp to stop it falling off: a typical machine for a Bulgarian to ride around Yambol, usually without a helmet of course. I noticed he was holding a crash helmet, and I could tell that he had mice in his home or garage. How did I know? The inner foam lining had been nibbled away and taken off somewhere for mouse-bedding. Exactly the same thing had happened with the crash helmet stored in my garage. After an exchange of greetings and a handshake, I asked how business was. He said there wasn't much around now summer had ended, but we agreed that that was good news.

He told me that this was a very exciting time for the fire brigade as they were expecting some new fire engines, and he went on to tell me about them. The fire engines they were using were now old and needed lots of servicing. Not a day went by when something had to be tinkered with or adjusted on these grand but ancient machines; but they were still good workhorses and did the job that they were intended to do. A couple of new modern fire engines were arriving from Germany, and the old ones would soon be decommissioned. I asked how old the current fire engines were; he said he didn't know, but he had been working there for thirty-two years and they were there when he arrived. When I asked about the new engines from Germany I found out that his idea of new was very different from mine; these were only twenty-two years old, he proudly confessed. Well that takes us back to 1985, and if I remember rightly, back in the UK fire engines haven't changed that much in style between then and now; I supposed the German type would certainly be in that league. We will see more of this friendly fireman now as he has promised to show me around the fire station and insisted he would take me up the lookout tower directly he found out I was scared of heights, the little devil! He added that my Lada was welcome to visit the fire station if it had a problem, as they currently have lots of time on their hands and would be happy to service it. The friendliness of these people never fails to overwhelm me! Would I have met him without Galia? Probably not!

SIMPLE TREASURE - 42

- A Lottery in Bulgaria -

We have a very good Bulgarian friend who lives and works in Yambol. Her job is managing a lottery hut and Galia and I had an invitation to check the place out and catch up with the news. These lottery huts are usually prefabricated stand-alone huts, in spots in the town centre walkways or in the centre of the huddles of high-rise apartments. Having passed these places many a time, I have only been inside one once with another Bulgarian friend who does the lottery weekly: he's only won once in five years, and then not much! The purpose of the lottery games is to subsidise sports in Bulgaria and many have 'Sport Lotto' in Cyrillic on the facade of the hut.

Of course, the lower the probability of winning, the bigger the cash prize is given. It is a matter of opinion though as to whether the lottery systems here are beneficial. As with these systems elsewhere in Europe, it is another 'tax on the poor', or as we used to call it in the UK an 'idiot tax'. There is not a lot of business generated, from what I can see and from what our Bulgarian lottery manager tells us, but then it is a National Lottery not a local one, which is why it carries on. The same system of having an option to pay tax before the draw or after applies here, but at only 5 stotinki most pay. Most think they are going to win every week anyway! The week we visited the jackpot was over 1,200,000 leva, for a stake of 40 stotinki plus 5 stotinki tax. That's some return for a win!

I entered the hut, stepping round our friend's bright green car, parked in its usual place — in typical Bulgarian fashion, halfway up the pavement and partly blocking the entrance to the lottery hut. It felt as though I was entering a betting office, and I expected the usual smoky atmosphere and litter, but this was far from the case. The odds and betting options were scattered around the iron-barred front window, but directly I crossed the atmosphere changed: there was a polished wooden cash desk with lovely scenic pictures around its window. On the shelf where you filled out your lottery card there were pot plants, and everywhere a feeling as though you were in someone's home. In the corner stood a bucket and mop, and a freestanding fan to cool customers while they filled in their ticket to potential riches. Ashtrays sparkled in the sun that peered in through the front window. It was no surprise that feeling of home was there, and our friend treats it exactly that way. No litter of used lottery cards on the floor, a spotlessly clean environment that made you feel very welcome.

All the time we were there, it must have been about an hour with all the talking we did, not one customer appeared, despite it being around five in the afternoon on a bright sunny day — a time when many people finish work and walk home. That did surprise me. Another day when we went there, we spent another hour talking, but it was a Saturday afternoon and the rush of customers throughout that hour was non-stop. That didn't curtail the talking that went on throughout our visit, with the lotto hopefuls joining in the chat as well of course; that was only natural, as that's their main hobby.

SIMPLE TREASURE - 43

- Small Talk -

In Bulgarian villages, where talking is the main pastime, a certain greeting is used more often than the usual 'Hello' or 'Hi' heard in the towns and cities — a leading question, and a sure sign that those Bulgarians who ask it want to spend time talking: 'What are you doing?' This greeting and question is put to me and countless others, and of course the natural tendency is to answer the question. The strange thing about this question is that it's never used to elicit information; it is used just as an introduction for an extended chat. It's usually obvious in most cases what you are doing at the time; even so, you still feel inclined to explain what you are doing, and so the talking starts. If I have just entered the village shop to buy bread and beer and a good neighbour is already there, who knows full well I go there at the same time on the same day to buy the same things, they'll still ask, 'What are you doing?' I of course explain that I am here in the shop to buy bread and beer, and the talking begins.

Talking about what they know already is a Bulgarian habit; for example, we will be eating some homemade village banitsas (Skalitsa Banitsas) and they will ask how it's made, even though they have been making the same banitsa in the same village to the same recipe every other day for decades. But still they ask. They will ask whether I am growing tomatoes in the garden, even though they have seen them and talked in depth about them only a few moments ago, even helped pick some for this evening's salad. But they still ask. They will enquire when am I going back to Yambol when they know week in week out I leave on

Sunday afternoon at the same time, and personally say goodbye to them at this time, and have for over a year now. But they still ask. The list of asking and talking about the obvious is endless, which is another reason why Bulgarians talk so much. So, to summarise the phrase 'What are you doing?': it's a Bulgarian form of greeting; it's not used to find out what you are doing (they already know); it's used to get to spend more even more time talking; it's a verbal device to stop you and them doing whatever you were doing; it's a Bulgarian trigger for everything to grind to a halt — again. In equation form, it would look something like this:

What are you doing? = (Obvious Answer + More Small Talk) – Work

SIMPLE TREASURE - 44

- Sofia Without Apples -

Galia and I spent some time in Sofia, Bulgaria's capital recently, killing time before a flight back to the UK. Sofia is a city with many attractions, but as I walked around it for some five hours I noticed that this city is lacking something. In those five hours, of the thousands of shops that we passed, four out of every five were fashion and jewellery shops. The vast majority of the remainder was made up of fast food joints, restaurants, cafes and casinos! It was with dismay that I peered into shop after shop with a total lack of interest in the contents displayed inside, which were essentially the fruits of materialism. In all that time, hypnotised by the repetition of similar shops, I did not see one single trader that sold fresh fruit or vegetables. In a country that has so much native produce, I found this staggering. The thousands of people working and living in the city were all eating on the move, cramming down pizzas, sandwiches or cakes as they go; it's is no wonder that eating habits are a concern in the Bulgarian cities. It seems that Sofia is obsessed with designer fashion and jewellery, and I was quite shocked at the narrow range of business lines based here. The population have money to throw away on this never ending supply of luxury goods, and you could spend a lifetime shopping, but you can't find an apple unless it is gold plated.

Why do I find this so upsetting? Everyone is tied to an economy based on wants rather than needs, especially so in cities like Sofia. Coming from non-materialistic village way of life on a smallholding and looking in, there is something morally wrong with Sofia City and the inaccessibility of a simple apple.

- Sofia City, Saturday Night -

We touched down on Bulgarian soil at 1:20 in the morning. The train to Yambol was due to depart at 6:30, so as we made our way to Sofia station Galia suggested we could spend the five hours until the train left in a cafe at the station, drinking coffee to stay awake. The taxi dropped us off at a very still and calm railway station. There were lights on in a cafe in the distance, so we rolled our cases noisily across the broken concrete pavements. We struggled to one station cafe and found five police officers sitting around drinking coffee, for the good reason that this cafe was only open to the police; and no other cafes were open until 6:00 that morning. We found ourselves out on the street for over four hours, laden with luggage, mingling with the denizens of the night: cab drivers touting for business, roaming gypsies and beggars, young drunks still full of vodka and rakia from their Saturday night out in Sofia. We parked ourselves by the large glass doors, within sight and earshot of the coffee-drinking police for a bit of insurance. I did seem as if these policemen (and one policewoman) were getting paid for drinking coffee all night, although later I was to realise that this wasn't the case.

Every ten or fifteen minutes a taxi would pull up, the driver would get out of the vehicle and walk towards us; and every time we knew what for. It was like a parade of parrots, who'd all been taught the same phrase: 'Where are you going?' 'Yambol,' we said, each time, and a figure was always given for the ride, which varied from 300 leva to 450 leva depending on the cheekiness of the cab driver. Their argument was always that we could be home by the time the train arrived here in Sofia.

We would quote the driver the cost for the train fare, 16 leva, and ask them whether they would pay an extra 300 leva for a couple of hours wait? They usually walked away at that point, deep in thought. After the first few we were getting a bit fed up, so we moved away from the taxi rank and turned our backs to oncoming cab drivers, which seemed to do the trick.

When we first got there we were only a couple of metres from a gypsy who sat on a small brick wall; he only had one leg and carried a crutch. He watched us for hours and we eventually thought that was he was waiting for an opportunity to steal something. It was only later that we realised he was waiting to go to work and had no home to go to: that was where he lived, sitting on the wall. We ended up talking to him; he was as nice as pie, as we gave him some cigarettes to keep him going. First impressions, eh? Another character turned up, whom we recognised from the plane; he was due to catch the same train as us, but was going on further to Burgas. In Bulgaria it's quite unbelievable how often you get talking to strangers, unlike where we had just come from.

This chap had gone to the UK because he had been told the streets were paved with gold. He didn't have a profession and went without any work permit or visa. His idea was that he would find work by word of mouth and earn cash in hand. After three months based in Peterborough he had found a job in a factory with an Egyptian manager, where he was paid £100 for working a 50-hour week. His digs were a three-by-four metre room, with no facilities and a shared kitchen and bathroom downstairs, for which he paid £30 a week rent plus bills. Food was extra, of course. He was back in Bulgaria now because all he had managed to save up in the three months before his visa expired was his airfare back to Sofia. His experience had been a reality check at the end of the day. The only money he had on him was a £10 note, which we exchanged for him, as the bureau de change didn't open until half an hour after his train left.

An elderly but quite slim and fit-looking man walked past us at one point, and I saw he had a baseball bat tucked into his belt. He stopped, and of course got talking to us: he had a story to tell, and he told it. A couple of hours ago there had been a gunfight only a hundred metres away in an underpass. A young armed drunk had been shot dead by the police. This was normal in the early hours of the morning, he told us. With the lack of work and money, many young people try the armed hold-up give-us-your-money trick, which sometimes works and sometimes doesn't. This time it hadn't, and he was dead. Which is a good enough deterrent for me, if not for others. The Sofia police force's policy appeared to be shoot first and ask questions later when it came to confronting someone with a gun.

'In any case,' asked our baseball-bat carrying friend, 'for what other reason would someone want to be carrying a gun in the early hours of the morning? There are no wolves here in Sofia city centre.' And he had a point. I asked what he was doing with a baseball bat. He said that it was to defend him against others with baseball bats. Funnily enough, moments later I saw a young man walk past, with another baseball bat in one hand and a woman in the other, looking a bit nervous as he walked past the coffee-drinking policemen and then us. But the police didn't seem too concerned; perhaps that is normal here, then.

Our next visitor was a drunk; he was about mid-twenties, with a shaven head, and looked more like a Russian than a Bulgarian due to his very pale complexion. Although not intimidating Galia or our friend who had been ripped off in England, we didn't make any eye contact with him. I found this hard to do as I thought it might cause offence; instead it led to conversation. Galia's suggestion that I didn't know any Bulgarian was a good one, so I pleaded ignorance at questions put to me. He soon got fed up with my 'I don't understand!' replies to everything. He slumped down to the ground and sat quietly for a few hours right next to us. Five o'clock arrived and the cafe opened early, as they saw some decent folk waiting outside: you don't look a gift horse in the mouth with business hanging around. The drunk followed us in and slumped down on a bench next to us, along with our Burgas-bound friend, who accepted a coffee from us and chatted to us the next half hour. Eventually the drunk woke up and asked if I could move to let him out; I had blocked him in on the narrow bench. He seemed quite shocked that I understood, but fortunately he was still too drunk to realise that I had been deliberately feigning ignorance earlier.

At last the railway station opened: too early for many, as it filled with yawning crowds on their way to work. We bought tickets and ate banitsas. They were old and cold, but still better than anything I had eaten in the UK in the last six months! We boarded the train: it left dead on time, and stress levels fell even further as we pulled out of the city. I hate cites generally, and Sofia is no exception, but despite its problems — gang warfare, gunfights, drinking and drug related crimes — its individualism stands out. It is not a carbon copy of the other cities I have visited, and is still distinctly Bulgarian in its manner and ways.

We had our tickets inspected twice on the four-hour journey. The ticket inspectors are very serious and never smile; they also come in pairs, a man and a woman, presumably for security reasons. Everyone has to have a ticket, whether first, second or third class, with a seat number on it, and you have to sit in that seat. Now the ticket inspectors may well be the reason for the lack of graffiti or vandalism in the train, as they scare the hell out of potential wrong-doers with their no-nonsense attitude. There was a young tough-looking Bulgarian chap who placed himself on a seat, had his ticket checked and punched, then after the inspector moved off decided to plonk himself down in the next empty seat. When the inspectors returned from their rounds they instructed the poor chap to move back to his original allocated seat. Jobs-worth, maybe, but I feel their justified in gaining discipline and respect. Not too dissimilar to the police here, who have respect mixed with fear, and it made us feel so much safer on the train in Bulgaria than ever we felt in the UK. Yambol hove into view, and the city of Sofia was left well behind us. The train journey had been so much cheaper and more pleasant than a taxi run!

SIMPLE TREASURE - 46

- Ladas and Rats -

Winter here in Bulgaria is short and sharp, and you should be well prepared for if you have a car. Now I have a Lada, and very proud of it I am, even though I hate cars. But this car has character, even though it seems to be a source of some embarrassment to many of my expatriate acquaintances.

With winter approaching, the Lada was meticulously prepared for its hibernation in my farmhouse garage. The battery was taken out and put on trickle charge (via a DIY solar charger, designed for AA rechargeable batteries, stuck on the kitchen windowsill — I wasn't quite sure whether this would work, but the idea was so Bulgarian I was glowing with pride that it was my own). I packed the car with blankets underneath the bonnet, over the front radiator grille and on top of the bonnet to insulate against the severe cold that was bound to come. It was snugger than a bug in a rug. Then the car was jacked up, front wheels raised off the ground in order for the tyres to be laid up to rest. The front tyres both have slow punctures (normal in Bulgaria) so this would ensure they were not crushed when totally devoid of air after a few days. The back wheels were blocked and the handbrake taken off to avoid stretching the cable. The fuel tank was run until judged to be almost empty as the preparations for the Lada's winter were complete. It was all very reassuring, as I was to be away throughout the winter months.

Arriving back at the end of winter the car was exactly as I had left it. The weather was warmer now, and the blankets and sheets were removed to reveal the engine after its hibernation. The flat front tyres were pumped up, and the car let down onto the concrete garage floor. The battery was lowered in and connected up, and the car sprung to life after about five turns of the engine: the improvised trickle-charging system for the battery had worked perfectly; the car was a goer, and within twenty minutes of being snugly tucked away it was ready for action. It was only three weeks later, when I took the car out during the night, that I discovered the lights didn't work!

The cause? I had covered the engine with blankets and sheets during winter, and this had made excellent nesting material for rats and mice. The next morning I took a closer look at the electrical system. Half of the plastic casing on the relay systems had been eaten, and the wiring stripped of its plastic coating. A fair few of the wires had been gnawed and even severed by rat teeth. It was no wonder the lighting didn't work.

SIMPLE TREASURE - 47

- Where is Maria? -

From the first time I came to live in Skalitsa, one family have always been a constant, to the degree that it feels as though I have become part of their family. Sasho, the man of the house has been my adopted honorary 'brother' for two years now and quite often we are in each others' houses to the early hours of the morning. All the things I have learnt about village life and country living have been courtesy of Sasho and Rosa, his school-teacher wife. I have lost count how many times we have been helped out by this family. Two years ago Rosa's father passed away — a very sad occasion, but he had had a good life and was at the age where many Bulgarian males do pass over to the other side. I saw him the day before he died, and this has stuck with me ever since. The sight of someone who you know will not be in this world for much longer brings to the forefront what is important in this life; quite a humbling experience, and one that makes you put your own problems into perspective.

Part of the family live in Ovchi Kladinets, the nearest neighbouring village to Skalitsa; Maria, Sasho's sister, and her husband live there. From the very first day I met Maria there was a sense of deep affection, and always a total joy to have her presence. Everyone has the same opinion of her — she is the kindest, most generous and sincere person that you could ever meet. Many times we have visited her in Ovchi Kladinets and been treated like close family. There has never been a time that we have left without a boot filled with garden produce and a big sloppy kiss goodbye. Maria is as big as her personality: loud, brash, uninhibited, speaking her mind at all times. She has a very broad sense of humour, which crosses many subject boundaries. She quite clearly has no scruples about anything. Without Maria this world would be a much poorer place, and never at any point did anyone ever conceive that she wouldn't be here.

On our return to Skalitsa, Rosa brought the shocking news that Maria was very ill and didn't have any chance of recovery. We couldn't believe that this woman, the life and soul of Bulgaria, and the same age as me, could ever have got this way. We offered to take Sasho and Rosa to the village, as they didn't have any transport, although we did dither, as Maria would try and get out of her death bed to cater for us and we didn't want to stress her further. But we decided to go, as we knew for sure that we would never see her again. On arrival we went in and I just didn't know that that was Maria sitting on the bed. It looked nothing like her. She had lost so much weight that she was unrecognisable. Her normal bubbly forceful tone had diminished into a whimper as we greeted her. Everyone was in tears, as the full impact of her illness became a reality before our very eyes.

The next hour or so was painful for everyone, as we knew that this was probably the last time we would see her. I won't go into detail about her illness, as it is complicated and not something that should be broadcast. We left with this picture in our heads, of a woman who had been in our hearts and heads for so long transformed into a woman just clinging on to life. How cruel can life be? This again makes us feel so guilty about anything and everything we complain about, how insignificant these problems are compared to what we see before us.

Maria passed away a few months later and we all miss here company and up-beat personality sorely. We all have to go at some point in our lives, but it's a tragedy that sometimes such wonderful people have to leave so early.

SIMPLE TREASURE - 48

- Food from Baba Mama -

I live with Baba now during the day. Galia is out to work early till late and I am writing, with Baba Mama doing her busy woman about the house act everyday. She is eighty-four and doesn't stop: back and forth, from chores in the kitchen to sweeping the yard, watering the garden to putting the washing out. She starts at 7:00 in the morning and doesn't stop until bedtime. There is a rest at around midday, when she gets her head down for a little snooze, but that's where it ends. Even when she is sitting down her hands are busy, sewing, knitting or repairing something.

What Baba can't understand is why I don't slow down and eat and sleep every couple of hours. She doesn't understand that a Bulgarian man is very different to an Englishman. I will always remember the time when she saw me vacuuming the front room: she was in tears, as she had never seen anything like it in her eighty-odd years in Bulgaria. I know now that every time the clock goes past midday she pokes her head around the corner of the kitchen area where I work; she doesn't ask me whether I'm hungry, she tells me I'm hungry. To be fair she probably knows; I start work before 8:00, so a fair morning's work has been done at this point. The first week this routine came into play Baba didn't get any sleep; she was too shy and humble to tell me that her usual sleeping sofa was being occupied by my posterior while I was tapping away on the laptop. Little did I know that I was ruining her routine, until Galia found out and told me one evening. Now I move into another room for the rest of the day to let her have a well-earned forty winks in peace; but not before she has prepared me food and drink, whether I want it or not.

Now Baba is an expert cook, and there isn't anything she prepares that isn't home-cooked and natural. Basic ingredients are all from the market or from my own Skalitsa farm. She is a superb cook and I cannot ever remember not liking anything she has prepared. Sometimes I'm a little wary about how long the food is kept, as Baba always uses the big pot to make huge batches — it's a question of economic cooking, energy-wise. There has often been food, meat at that, which has been standing around for four or five days. This used to worry me immensely at first — was it my own British standards that have brainwashed me into thinking that everything has be eaten within two days or you'll die writhing in the throes of food poisoning? Yes, now I think it was a commercial ploy by global food producers to make you buy more, putting the fear of God into you if you didn't!

I digress. Baba has come to accept that the microwave we bought for her has its uses. It took her almost a year to come to terms with it and understand what she can and can't put into it; and that was from experimentation, not instruction! Now she can't get enough of it, and the little bottled-gas stove, used religiously before, is now redundant most days, used only for the original cooking using the big pot. From the big pot single portions go onto a plate and into the microwave, and she is now a dab hand at this. Today for the third day running and the fifth meal we had chicken, bean and potato stew, a meal that never in a million years would I ever get bored with. The bones, as after every meal, are given to Alex, our neighbour's doorbell dog.

Each day Baba lays the table and never a day goes by without raw garlic, fresh bread and a green salad complement the main dish; the most delicious combination with any meal. Drink accompaniment is ayran made from yoghurt made in Skalitsa from my neighbour's fresh cow's milk. Baba loves ayran along with all three generations of family living here. Spoilt? Yes, but in this day and age of fast food how lucky I am to get traditional food served up by the most respectful and experienced cook. She is handing something down to me, and long may it continue. Baba has such a variety of cooking skills and recipes that now, after a while of Bulgarian routine; the siesta habit after lunchtime meals is beginning to have an effect on me. A lie down after her fantastic food is something that just seems so natural to do. My habits of a lifetime, picked up in England — not taking breaks, skipping meals — were finally beginning to be laid to rest. Thank you, Baba, for showing me the way.

SIMPLE TREASURE - 49

- Lada Tyres -

From day one of buying my Lada it's been a source of some worry or other. The steering was faulty and I feared it would be costly to fix it. Every time I turned there was a big bump and the steering wheel just bumped and over-steered. This happened in both directions — the car still went left and right, just suddenly! Added to this the steering was very stiff, giving me Popeye-style workouts whenever I drove. It was especially hard in the Yambol streets, home of the three-point turn. Throughout the two years of owning the car this was something I put up with. I regarded it as part and parcel of the Lada driving experience. I even had other Bulgarians assess the problem, and their sharp intake of breath at the thought of the cost of repairs always seemed to confirm my suspicions. So it was left: as long as I could steer the car, which was the prime objective.

The last year or so both front types constantly leaked air. Every few days I made a trip to a garage to pump them up again. I put off getting them repaired: the tyres had good tread, they worked, the air in the garages was free, and so it carried on. This is how it is in Bulgaria, anything to save money; as long as it works but doesn't cost anything, even if it is a little inconvenient to keep it working, that's how it will stay. Finally it was time to get the tyres seen to, initially with a view of repairing the existing tyres as we had a little spare cash. We estimated that this should only cost a maximum of 20 leva for both, but I knew from the bulges on its wall that at least one of the tyres was beyond repair. They had been in this state from day one, but the car had rolled on regardless, and got us to places. We looked at the cost of tyres many times and just the thought of the cost put us off doing anything about it, until Galia spotted some very cheap tyres in a supermarket one day. We checked the existing tyres sizes on the car and found they were 185 (whatever that meant). The equivalent size was found in the supermarket, at 75 leva each. Before committing to buy them we thought we would check whether the old ones could be repaired.

Galia's son recommended a particular garage opposite the fire station, so on recommendation we checked it out. Dimtar, the owner, was busy fixing a child's motorbike he had imported from England. He took of our front tyres off, and it was quite obvious they couldn't be repaired: it was no wonder they were losing air, the rubber was fractured in numerous places and the heads of three or four nails protruded from the tread. Added to all this they were the wrong-sized tyres for a Lada. His recommendation was two new tyres, both the correct size for the vehicle. Was this a classic Bulgarian trick, hoodwinked us into buying two new tyres? We held our breath, waiting to find how much he was going to charge. We breathed again when he revealed the cost: 64 leva for each tyre, fitted, balanced and ready to roll. We agreed and they were set up within twenty minutes. And what a close shave it was, nearly buying the wrong size tyres again. The biggest joy and relief was the steering problem — it's completely disappeared. Maybe the right size tyres had something to do with it!

SIMPLE TREASURE - 50

- Working Bulgarians -

Workers in Bulgaria are subjected to very long hours indeed; not only long hours, but also many months without holiday entitlement and ridiculous rates of pay. But all is not what it seems. We had got to the point where because of the stress of living and working in England we returned early without much money, so working here again is something we now have to do. Having worked in Bulgaria before, and put the hours in at a Bulgarian rate of pay, the problem was that I worked like an Englishman and my pace of work was completely different from the Bulgarians. Long hours — up to 12 hours a day — are quite normal for Bulgarian workers; the pace at which they work means that they tackle the problem of extended hours via slow, methodical work with many breaks. Sometimes working is just a case of them being there for most of the time. I have lost count of the times I see workers in shops and markets just sitting there, smoking or talking. This is quite normal: the customers and shoppers are far outnumbered by the sellers and shopkeepers, so busy times are nonexistent.

The minimum rate of pay per month in Bulgaria is around 220 leva each month. Based on working an eight-hour, five-day week, this is 1.38 leva (55p) an hour. Most people, however, work in excess of ten hours over six days, which brings the true hourly rate down to 92 stotinki (37p) an hour. Bear in mind also that the majority of workers are paid the minimum wage, and there is a black market where less than this is paid to casual workers. A packet of cigarettes now costs on average around 2.40 leva, and would take over two and a half working hours to earn. In the

UK it would take just one hour, based on their national minimum wage! So who says that cigarettes are cheap in Bulgaria? They are nearly three times the equivalent here for the working Bulgarians. I won't go into how smoking pensioners get by...

The point I am trying to get over is that long working hours are something that is normal here, and are only regarded with shock by foreigners comparing western European hours and pay. Because they are in the workplace for ten hours or so the term work may not apply for the whole of that time. So, because of our relative poverty, Galia now has to work. Relatively speaking though, she is better off than most other Bulgarian workers, as I would not allow her to work through the sixty-hours-a-week barrier on a minimum wage, although she has before and would have again if I hadn't been there. For myself, I was offered work driving long distances but Galia insisted that I didn't take it up as I was English: she knew full well that my work-rate would be a hundred and ten per cent, not like a Bulgarian, and I would totally exhaust myself doing it. She is right of course!

SIMPLE TREASURE - 51

- A Bulgarian MOT -

It was long overdue, in fact four months overdue and about time it was done. We had got away with it since we had been back in Bulgaria, but getting away with it in this part of the world is normal. I'm talking about the Bulgarian equivalent of the MOT test and certificate. It wasn't that long ago that my C90 Honda moped I used in England went through the test and failed because one of the tyres was fitted the wrong way round. I had to spend £40 on getting the bugger swapped around and then retested! No leeway, advice or help, but purely a device for making more money out of people.

Back in Bulgaria such instances are unheard of. Yes, they do have a predisposition for ridiculous amounts of documentation: this will always be the case here, not just because of the ex-communist infrastructure but also due to the Bulgaria's recent membership of the EU, who seem to make it their business to complicate processes to ridiculous lengths, with mandatory paperwork and accountability for all. Nothing is easy in this world of red-tape and bureaucracy that causes so much frustration and systems to grind to a halt. In fact it is my opinion that much of this complicated paperwork is put there to put the general public off entering into said transactions or services.

I digress! The problem with my Lada car was that none of the lights were working, due to rats turning the engine compartment into a temporary home and gnawing through all the electrical circuits. Who in their right mind would even consider putting a vehicle through an MOT in view of this? Galia's suggestion was to just not mention the fact — she was sure that all was going to be okay, as it was last year when the tyres were bald. We arrived at the garage at lunchtime, and somewhat inevitably it was shut; we were told to come back in an hour. A Bulgarian hour, as oft mentioned, quite often isn't an hour, so we turned up two days later, as advised! We had all the documentation except the full registration document, which was in Skalitsa. He remained adamant he couldn't issue the MOT certificate without this document. Luckily we were on our way to Skalitsa, so we made our way there and returned in the pouring rain.

Ivan, the mechanic, asked me to put my car on the service pit in the garage, and I drove it over the metal-lined pit with a sense of foreboding. Was he going to conduct a full test on the car? Had Bulgarian MOT procedures now come into line with other EU directives? Was Galia's assumption that it would be okay just wishful thinking? Once the car was parked and dripping into the pit Ivan began completing the tick list of items to be tested, but without even a slight glimpse at the car. Within five minutes the 30 leva had been paid (it was 15 leva last year!) and the certificate had been signed, sealed and delivered! All that remained was to stick the certificate on the inside of my front windscreen, and that's when I realised why he wanted my car up on the ramp in the garage: It was raining outside and he didn't want to get wet when putting the sticker on the car! Why on earth did I doubt that anything would be any different this year in Bulgaria, apart from the cost? Last year Ivan didn't even look at the car before signing the pass certificate; this year was exactly the same. So even without any lights working it passed, I suspect because it was a Lada and we spoke Bulgarian. Shortly after this I spoke to another Brit who had been living here for five years; he complained that his car had to go through a meticulous test to pass its MOT, and he had no end of trouble getting his certificate. There were probably two points that weren't in his favour: his car wasn't a Lada, and he didn't speak a word of Bulgarian!

SIMPLE TREASURE - 52

- Another Bulgarian Door -

It had been quite a while since my new Bulgarian door was fitted to my Skalitsa farmhouse, but the project still wasn't completed, true to Bulgarian form. Mind you it wasn't paid for at the time anyway. The month of May brings about much warmer weather, and this brings the flies to life. The problem is keeping them out of the house. The only way in is through the front door, as all the windows have fly screens fitted — one of the great inventions of modern day living here. We had intended to fit a fly screen when the door was put in, but nobody got around to doing it. We now had time to get this organised, especially with paying guests now regularly staying, and some due in the next few days. So off we went to see Kosta, the manager of the metalwork factory opposite the mayor's house. Kosta wasn't there, but we saw a worker and gave instructions for the door to be made up and fitted before our guests arrived. A slight feeling of foreboding came over me when he cheerily said 'No problem!' As from much experience as anything: this comment is usually a signal for future problems.

The next day two cars pulled up outside my house: Kosta, and one of his workers who had a fly screen tied to his car roof. Within ten minutes the door had been fitted and an explanation given to its operation. It had been secured onto the existing door, but couldn't close due to the protruding handle — only one door could be opened at a time. So when the front door was shut the fly screen had to be left open and when the fly screen was shut the front door had to be open. A small design fault, but being Bulgarian it still did the job of keeping flying insects out. The job was done and Kosta the boss insisted that he didn't want any money, as it was a gift. I couldn't accept that and literally forced a 20 leva note upon him. As the front door had to remain open when the fly screen was shut there was the problem of the door slamming against the wall when the wind caught it. To solve this Galia suggested a Bulgarian solution of sticking Brillo pads to the wall! Although a strange sight, this idea seemed as though it would work, so off we went to Maria's shop to get a couple of pan scrubbers. We used glue to stick them to the wall, and very proud we were of solving a problem Bulgarian-style. What would our English guests think of it though? So we have a working system in place and peace of mind that flies will not become a persistent problem in our farmhouse during this long summer. That is if we remember to shut the door each time.

SIMPLE TREASURE - 53

- A Bulgarian Van -

We had a big problem when we had to buy a sofa bed for additional guests staying at our farmhouse in Skalitsa; they wanted 35 leva to deliver the sofa to Skalitsa, and Galia wasn't having any of it. The sofa was just too big to put on the Lada's roof, although if I were a gypsy it would have fitted quite easily, with room for another one! The idea of borrowing her brother's van came up to save money of course. We arranged to pick up the van a few days later when the sofa was ready for collection. The cost of gas would amount to 15 leva, as her brother knew exactly how many kilometres to the litre it did. So we arrived at Galia's brother's factory to pick up the van. I hadn't seen it before, so when I was shown it by one of the workers I was quite excited. There, sitting parked in a field was a tatty old sky-blue transit van. It must have been about fifteen years old, and had character written all over it. Big enough for a sofa for sure, but I was looking forward to driving this typical old-style Bulgarian workhorse.

First we had to see how it worked; upon inspection of the rear doors we saw not the original lock but a front door handle and lock, with a Yale key to open and shut it. A small twist of wire held the handle down so it didn't fly open during transit. Inside were empty oil canisters covered with old flattened cardboard boxes — the cargo area. The driving area was a maze of DIY inventions added to keep the systems working. There was no ignition key: it had been hotwired and converted to a push-button to start the engine and a flick switch to turn it off. The clutch was shin-level off the floor, and you had to raise your whole leg to get on top of it to disengage. The floor was missing in places, and here and there ground could be seen. The gears were on the right of the steering wheel, and with each gear change there was grating noise, not too dissimilar from nails on a blackboard but about forty decibels louder.

The light switches were homemade, screwed onto the dashboard with the aid of another odd bit of plastic. The instrument panel was an exercise in redundancy — the speedometer didn't work, the milometer didn't show any signs of life and the trip meter was having the day off. The fuel indicator was at zero, so I can only assume this didn't work either. Judging the temperature of the oil was impossible, as, yes, this didn't work either. And there, just to the left on the window screen, was an up-to-date MOT sticker! Well being a Bulgarian van the most essential piece of equipment was working perfectly — the radio! It was finely tuned to Radio Veselina and blared out Bulgarian folk-pop music as we moved off. Apart from the fact that noise of the gear changes wasn't quite drowned out by the radio the van worked perfectly, and got us to and from where we wanted to go for exactly the estimated 15 leva for the gas. Half the price of the delivery service we were first offered. But what price can you put on the experience?

SIMPLE TREASURE - 54

- Two Bulgarian Restaurants -

It's not often that we go to a restaurant. Don't think for one moment it is because we don't enjoy dining out — on the contrary, we love it. In fact it is quite a rare occasion that we venture out to eat, drink and dance. There are numerous reasons for this; firstly, and probably the most obvious reason in the eye of our prudent Galia, is the cost. Relatively speaking it is peanuts to pay, and sometimes some menu items are actually cheaper than making your own. But you still feel that you have to order additional accompaniments with most individual menu items and that's where economy leaves the building. In recent times we haven't had peanuts to give, and if we did we'd probably have eat them! It actually leads to us not really enjoying the restaurant moments, being very conscious of the money being paid out for a luxury we can ill afford. It is quite common for me to see Galia looking at the menu with her finger running down the price on the right, not reading the description of the dish. Invariably it is not always the cheapest that is chosen but the best value for money — there is a big difference.

The other reason for not eating out is quite often the hassle factor, and after a long day at work the preparation for going out is not easy, especially for a Bulgarian woman, who has a dress and a look for every occasion. Not only that, her advice given to her Englishman invariably takes just as long, as I change into one outfit only to be told another one should be worn. This particular evening we had decided to go out to eat. We had just been paid and probably for the first time since living in Bulgaria we were optimistic about our financial future. This was enough to justify a decision to go out, even though we were both very tired after a long working week. As mentioned, it is very rare that we go out, and even rarer that just the two of us go alone. This evening was to be no exception, as we were expecting Galia's son Anton and his partner Koyna to join us later.

Off we went, treading through the cobblestone streets of Yambol on a slightly overcast evening. The breeze had a feel of rain about it, but undeterred we cantered on to our destination: the Chinese restaurant in the town centre. Not our number one choice by any means: for a start it wasn't Bulgarian, but the food-to-cost ratio put it high in the rankings as a good value venue. As we walked on we spotted another restaurant we hadn't been to before: 'The Bulgaria Restaurant'. Never having really noticed it before, Galia suggested we try it. She hadn't been there for at least five years, so we entered and took a seat in the garden section, even though the rain threatened. Soon rakia and shopska salad arrived on the table, alongside a barbecued Serbian-style kyufte and sautéed potatoes that had been subjected to a profusion of Bulgarian herbs. The trouble with excellent food is not just that you want to eat — you want to eat it all, immediately. The temptation to do exactly that was getting the better of me, but Galia was Bulgarian and had a lifetime of experience in nibbling rather than stuffing.

An hour had disappeared and so had all the food and drink. Anton and Koyna were still nowhere to be seen; what should we do? Well in this society you are free to do what you want without being criticised or singled out, so there was only one real option: 'Another rakia and shopska salad please!' was the request to the waitress, who was single-handedly dealing with every aspect of the restaurant, including the cooking! I don't know how she managed, but I do know she will be on minimum wage! This was definitely not a case of not being able to get the staff nowadays. Ten o'clock arrived and I was tickling the last remnants of the second shopska with my fork; still no Anton and Koyna! We thought about ringing them to say we were going home to bed; we were dozing off into the shopska at this point. Not only that, the wind had a chill to it as darkness fell upon Yambol, and we were full, frustrated and freezing!

It was decided that when they did turn up we'd go somewhere else. The food was brilliant, but we'd had enough, and the place lacked Bulgarian atmosphere: Michael Jackson, Abba, Elton John and Queen had all taken their third encore of the evening. We missed the Bulgarian music, and it actually put a dampener on the evening. The crowds had dispersed, either towards home or further into town, where the nightclub scene was about to start. It was almost 10:30 and the guys finally arrived, but this is Bulgaria and it's normal for people to turn up over two hours late. Trying to find the waitress took a full ten minutes, as she was busy preparing a delicious-looking dessert. Pudding in one hand, she rang up our bill with the other.

What were we to do now? We were bursting at the seams and Anton and Koyna hadn't eaten since lunchtime. Another restaurant, or find a bar or nightclub that serves food, or more to the point salad? What was about to happen was a bit of bad luck and good fortune at the same time! Now Anton, Galia's son, is very wilful, with a typical Bulgarian male streak right through him. He is an expert on many things — if you have a problem or want advice, he's straight in there with the answer, but in true Bulgarian style, while very convincing, it's maybe not always the best advice. Once we were in the town centre we looked at the Chinese restaurant, but it was a full- blown, deep-fried eating-, the thought just made us feel sick so we walked on by and came to a neighbouring night club, with a troop of bouncers. All five were dressed in pristine black shirts, adorned with flashing neon name-tags. Anton tried communicating with the leader of the troop. They looked quite intimidating from a distance, but in my experience when you speak to these guys they are as nice as pie: bored shitless and welcoming of any activity other than just standing there getting bored with each other.

Anton and I were invited to go into the club and check it out for the girls. A red carpet led us some twenty metres up a corridor to big, black, arched door, its impressive gold-plated fittings polished so they shone in the light from the chandeliers; it felt as though we were entering a royal palace. What is it about Bulgarian doors? There is such a big variety in this country. The sight before us, as the door slowly edged open was a room full of glitter.

It was a big circular room, with a long curved bar to match; everywhere you looked was seductively lit, and around half the perimeter of the ballroom-style floor was another continuous bar, with a row of bar stools silhouetted against the fluorescent blue wall. The music was loud but unobtrusive; conversations could take place here, but we had doubts about whether the sound levels would remain at fifty decibels later in the evening. The other strange thing about this place was it was empty! This is not unusual, as the crop of young and old pumpkins usually don't arrive until after midnight and stay until breakfast is served in the neighbouring twenty-four-hour banitsa bakery across the road. Anton and I looked at each other and a nod of the head was exchanged between us. Yes, we both agreed, this most definitely wasn't the place for us! Why? When we asked whether they served salad the short answer was, 'No!' How can you drink rakia without salad? Didn't they know anything about Bulgarian tradition here?

We all traipsed back along the red carpet, the bouncers entertained by our reasons for leaving. They really are the nicest people, these Bulgarian bouncers, although you do have to look beyond their exterior to find this out, and not many do. Next stop was the Apollo, an old and favourite haunt, last visited nearly two years earlier. It was locked, with no sign of life. The quest continued: the next venue was the basement room under the Tundzha Hotel, live music and dancing, but also very full. A stone's throw across the main road, another basement restaurant — more live music and dancing, with enough Bulgarian-style atmosphere to die for, but again, as we cut our way through the party scene it became quite apparent that there were no tables for us. On other occasions they would bring another table in for you, but this time there was absolutely no space to put it. We reluctantly retreated back outside into the lit streets of Yambol, the antiphonal sound of the relentless Bulgarian traditional music drifting all around us. We crossed the road, past the street with the Dublin Bar, a place I really don't like for so many reasons. The Piano Bar, far too up-market for our simple Bulgarian family group, and the cost in mind again of course — habits of a lifetime die hard.

Another basement bar/restaurant, and a loud, actively-dancing crowd greeted us as we opened the frosted double doors. This was more like a dance club, the music was noticeable more than anything else: Bulgarian chalga, folk-pop and traditional folk music ruled here. It sounded good, but there was another choice waiting for us a block on. Now you may think that all this touring round and failing to find a suitable place was bad luck, but it had its benefits. We had been walking for nearly an hour and with all the calories we had burnt the signs of hunger were beginning to creep up on us again. As each place was rejected it was more of a relief for Galia and me, as another walk was a fine solution to our previous gut-busting predicament. So we ventured out again to try Anton's new idea, and after a short walk we arrived at yet another door with a difference.

A flight of anonymous concrete steps doubled back on themselves down to a basement, stopping abruptly before an unusual door: unusual because it didn't have any character. This had to be the place for us after so much dilly-dallying in the streets of Yambol. Another set of double doors opened in front of us and the ingredients were all there to savour. A large group of locals, music, dancing, Bulgarian food and the whole place done out in traditional decor — all original, none of the pastiche or spoofed thematic rubbish you find in some bars (I won't mention the Dublin Bar!) There was a table for four in the distance begging us to take it. Typically glamorous young waitresses floated around like busy bees to the honey pot tables. The third salad of the evening, not a shopska but a cabbage salad served in a large bowl, which would last the duration. Another rakia and beers all round and we were now settled for the night. There was interest all round here, not least the Bulgarian artefacts surrounding us. A stuffed owl sat right next to us, watching proceedings.

Looking around there were many dead birds perched on the walls, watching the party unfold. This is a common sight in many bars and restaurants in Bulgaria, naturally so, as they love their hunting here.

Beautiful as most of these creatures are, they are shot not for food but ironically for wall decorations, from where they get see people tucking into their relatives, the poor chickens! The people around us were the most interesting, from all levels from young to old, intelligent to the dim-witted — all manner of Bulgarian life was here. In the corner another bouncer: his insurance is his looks. You wouldn't entertain making trouble with this guy as he made his presence felt with his physique. I swear his muscle-bound biceps had a bigger girth than my thighs, and with cyclist's legs I'm not slim! It's kind of reassuring though. The dancing encompassed all styles: who says you need to be able to dance, as I saw the stumbling going on. Luckily the Bulgarian traditional dance has a failsafe method (designed for non-dancers) where all participants hold each other's hands. This way if you stumble the dancers on either side holds you up. The steps don't really matter to some; it's the taking part that counts.

The dancing around the tables carried on all night. There was a Bulgarian DJ and what a character he was. A magic beer bottle, always re-filling itself, was his constant companion, along with a vodka bottle he tapped into every so often. He loved his job, dancing away behind his desk, singing and giving a running commentary throughout the evening. The later it got on the more agitated and extrovert he became — a showman to the last. The music was varied, but mostly Bulgarian: the DJ's choice, plus a few requests from the floor.

By the side of the dance floor a drummer was banging out some live percussion. The Bulgarian music mainly consists of one type of beat, and the whole evening this drummer, a small man but growing in stature with each drink, was getting more 'into the groove' with each passing song. Eventually the atmosphere overcame him, and he gradually shuffled his drum kit onto the dance floor to take a more central role in the party. There was a spotlight in the centre of the floor, and he made a beeline towards it a couple of times a before being ushered back by the restaurant manager. Hogging the dance floor, he reminded me of the over-keen Band Master on parade in The Dirty Dozen. Immersed in the distraction of looking around at all these characters and taking in the atmosphere, my part in the evenings socialising and discussion was minimal. I was too caught up in, on this rare night out in Yambol, amongst the scenes and experiences, the sudden realization that this was my new home.

- A Memorable Bulgarian Meal -

Another day, another culinary adventure — it's always a guessing game trying to discover what Baba is going to present at lunchtime. There are often clues the evening before, where she sometimes spends hours sitting outside in the garden or in the back room, preparing natural ingredients for the next day's meals. Whether it's peeling potatoes, mincing meat, sorting the beans, stripping the garlic, chopping the onions or countless other cook's chores, this gives the first clue. Ingredients are always prepared the evening before. The second part of the detective work is the smell in the kitchen mid-morning. The cooking would have been started early on and the aromas waft around the house, just like that trail in the Bisto Gravy advert during the 1970s. It isn't very hard to put both clues together and not be far off the mark.

Today I knew that there were some peas involved, as the previous evening Baba's daughter-in-law was in the garden with her, helping with shelling the peas picked that evening. Galia and I had collected them and brought them home from the grounds of the factory where Galia works. They grow a diverse selection of fruit and vegetables there, which are harvested and supplied to the workers and their families. What's more, having been there on a daily basis to drop off or collect Galia, I knew that all the food produced on that 'factory farm' is chemical free. So, organic peas were on the menu for sure, but what else? There was a distinct smell of something stewing that next morning, something meaty and wholesome for certain. Baba had never disappointed in the food stakes here, ever.

There was a call of 'Martin, munja!' Lunch was ready. The table for two was already laid as usual: matched pairs of cutlery, napkins and glasses, and whole bulbs of raw garlic, also from the factory farm, were dished out to Baba's enthusiastic commentary about how good it is for you. Glasses of freshly-made ayran were poured out. Knowing where the food had come from, and the knowledge that not one chemical is contained within, is a major contribution in the enjoyment of food and drink in Bulgaria. This particular ayran was made from sheep milk brought back from Skalitsa village and turned into homemade yoghurt in Yambol, then mixed with water and salt, producing the most wonderful ayran you could ever imagine and complementing the garlic sitting beside it perfectly. The bread, again daily made in Yambol, has to be bought daily as it goes off quickly in the warm Bulgarian weather and the absence of preservatives. Two days maximum for local bread here, the second day Baba uses the old bread to dip into her daily dose of linden tea. So we had ayran, garlic and bread; so far so good.

The main dish was about to be served and I wasn't quite sure what to expect. When it did arrive it was certainly different to anything I had seen before. Yes, there were peas, but in an amount I had never seen before — a whole large soup dish, full of peas as a bed for the chicken. The peas were used just like rice and the local herbs and chicken stock it was cooked in were spectacular in so many senses: smell, sight and taste all combined into a very memorable lunch. The chicken was a previous resident of Skalitsa, one from my own farm. I knew its history, therefore this completed a meal that remained totally free of any additive, preservative or whatever they put in we don't know about. The combinations of tastes hit the mark, although it wasn't complicated food, just very basic simple ingredients, combined into a feast for the senses. Baba had inspired yet again! Another lesson in how simple food can be so successful.

SIMPLE TREASURE - 56

- Malomir Liqueur Recipe -

My trip one weekend to see some Bulgarian friends in the neighbouring village of Malomir was memorable for many reasons; this was one of them. Amongst the usual food and drink put out for us, what looked like a vinegar bottle was placed on the table. The contents, as I was to find out, were not vinegar, and after being offered a glass of the rose-coloured liquid, I discovered it to be a liqueur, and a great discovery. The recipe was asked for, and the Baba Mama hostess explained there was no family secret attached to it. This was in turn made in my own village of Skalitsa, with my own homemade supplies, and it was found to be just as good. It does naturally retain the Malomir name though.

Ingredients (measures for 1-litre batches are given but this can be doubled, tripled or quadrupled for larger batches):

700 ml homemade wine (white or rose)
200 ml homemade sliva (plum) rakia
1 kg sugar
3 drops of vanilla essence

Preparation: put all the ingredients into a 2- or 3-litre plastic bottle and shake gently until all the sugar has been dissolved. You can place the filled bottle in a bowl of warm water for 15 minutes before shaking to help the process. Leave standing overnight and check in the morning that there is no sugar left in the base of the bottle. If there is, shake again and leave to stand for another 24 hours. Re-bottle the clear liqueur into airtight clean glass container(s) and store for two weeks in a cool dark place before drinking, accompanied by an ice cube or two.

Notes: The wine and rakia used in this liqueur has to be homemade country wine and rakia, as the wine and rakia from commercial suppliers give an inferior taste and poor end result! (This is local Bulgarian advice.)

SIMPLE TREASURE - 57

- A Funny Thing About Gabrovo -

During my work and research into cities, towns and villages in Bulgaria I come across some fascinating stories about places: this is one of them. The first I heard of Gabrovo was when a contestant from the town appeared on a Bulgarian TV show. He was a playboy character, and very different indeed to the other contestants; stinginess and selfishness was also part of his character, and needless to say he was a likable rogue, which did him no harm in the popularity stakes. Gabrovo is situated at the foot of the central Balkan Mountains, in the valley of the Yantra River, and is well known as an international capital of humour and satire. Throughout Gabrovo's long history it was deemed a great privilege for a child to be born there. Why? After I researched more about the town and its people, and discovered that the people of Gabrovo are reputed to be the best at moneysaving and bargaining. It is said that economy runs in their veins and they know instinctively how to get something for nothing. These are invaluable lessons taught by their ancestors, which is why it is regarded as such a privilege to be born there. At the sniff of a crisis they automatically switch into humorous mode, for it is said they have no alternative.

Internationally famed, many anecdotes are told about these shrewd and exceptionally prudent people. It is these anecdotes that originally started the phenomenon of Gabrovo humour, and they remain funny and relevant and to the Gabrovo citizen as vital as ever. The symbol of Gabrovo is a black cat with its tail being cut off — the story goes that was that the townsfolk cut the tails off their cats so when they let them out at night they could close the door faster and save heat. Gabrovo people also fit taps to their eggs, to save on the quantities of egg used for a soup; a whole egg seems too much to them to waste in soup. They stop their clocks to save wear on the cogwheels.

A favourite Gabrovo trick is to place green spectacles on their donkeys' noses: then when they feed them shavings the donkeys think they're eating hay. If they invite people to tea, which is rare in Gabrovo anyway, they heat the knives so the guests can't take any butter. Another common activity is saving money on chimneysweeps by throwing a cat down the chimney. It's generally regarded as a fact that when something new has only just hit the headlines somewhere, it has invariably already been done in Gabrovo. So if ever you are in Gabrovo you may want to visit the House of Humour and Satire.

SIMPLE TREASURE - 58

- The Fat of the Land -

Living in Bulgaria can present an idyllic lifestyle, where everything you want in life can be found: the countryside, coast and mountains; good food and drink; and health. Too much of a good thing is said to be bad, perhaps in terms of food and drink; and this is a prime example of a current trends in Bulgaria. Do we as foreigners here fall into the lure of the abundance of food, drink and the sedate lifestyle? If you do, you may want to read about the way things are here. Perhaps it's the European or even American food culture, primed to invade Bulgaria. They have their foot well and truly in the door now, with fast-food joints and supermarket convenience foods playing an increasing role in the Bulgarians' diet. This is becoming a problem, now it has been confirmed that half of Bulgarians are overweight. This is mainly due to a poor diet and an inactive life. What is more disturbing is that the thirty per cent of Bulgarians that are overweight are not even aware of their designation, as it's considered not only a privilege but strangely a measure sex appeal to be the proud owner of a beer belly in Bulgaria. As they say here, 'The bigger the rock, the bigger the snake!'

Men seem to be more prone to obesity than women, and this may be aided and abetted by a culture where women run around to feed their men, who have had a lifetime of being waited upon. Only ten per cent of the population are engaged in active vocations, with the rest, mostly the men, leading a sedentary life. Life begins at forty takes on a new meaning, as the weight factor gathers momentum for many adults beyond this age: with their metabolism slowing down, their eating habits often remain in the fast lane, not adjusting at all to account for this.

Strange but true, most overeating takes place in the poorest communities; this is a paradox. The inclination is for obesity to be more apparent in the Bulgarian Greek and Turkish communities, as opposed to the mainly trim figures of the Roma population, probably due to genetic factors. Also, in village life you will find a far more overweight population than in cities and towns; perhaps too much of the good life, a surplus of food and drink that costs next to nothing to produce, is responsible. It is not for any foreigner to tell a Bulgarian what they can or can't eat, or when to eat it — they have their own ideas about their diets and eating timetables, and they will stick to them. So an overweight population is now part of the culture within Bulgaria, due to bad eating habits, but hasn't this been the case throughout Europe and America?

Many Bulgarians eat what tastes good rather than what is good for them, with fried and salty food, combined with much wheat-based bread, being the main culprits. Over the last half-century in Bulgaria the rate of food consumption has risen seven-fold, and drinking quadrupled in volume over the same period. In European rankings Bulgaria is the runner-up in dietary-related heart disease (Russia is top). Even more serious are the implications for the new generation of Bulgarians — the kids! It is another fact that Bulgarians view children that are fat as healthy; in fact, the fatter the healthier, and mothers adjust their children's diets accordingly. Many mothers give their children fast food as their main diet: chips, hamburgers and pizza, accompanied by many sugar-based drinks, sweets and chocolate. These foods are extensively advertised on terrestrial Bulgarian television, and this doesn't help matters. The bandwagon of junk food advertising is now well established, with the obvious market of a new generation of Bulgarians. A testament to this is the fact that Bulgarian children are on average the fourth fattest in the world, after the Greek, English and Irish! The most important and healthy time for eating is breakfast, but in Bulgaria this is usually a cigarette and a coffee and a banitsa — or no food at all! (You would be amazed at how many Bulgarians I know who do this.)

Over thirty per cent of younger Bulgarians opt for meat and fried food for dinner: the worst food and the worst time to eat it. This alone is a recipe for obesity. The only way this can be turned around is by introducing dietary awareness through education, perhaps through a curriculum dedicated to this within schools, promoting public awareness through the media and enforcing strict moderation of advertising. This, however, is not a priority in Bulgaria's political circles at the moment, and it may take further alarming statistics on the effects of obesity for this to raise its head as a major issue in Bulgaria. This is a topic that has really made an impression on me. I recall coming here three years ago, when there was only one supermarket in Yambol town. Away from this supermarket, I wasn't really aware of anybody being noticeably overweight. This supermarket was situated in a highly populated area, surrounded by blocks of flats. As you approached the supermarket it was a bit like entering a freak show. The reason for this seemed so blatant as to be bizarre — I can only put it down to supermarket-led diets in the area; the local population brought to their knees by marketing tactics!

As a foreigner in Bulgaria, with a good health education and knowledge of what is considered a good diet, it is very hard to get

Bulgarians to see it any other way than their own. It is also very difficult to stick to your own dietary habits without insult, to a certain degree, the hospitality given to foreigners in Bulgaria. There is a danger of falling into the hospitality trap, and suddenly finding out you're several sizes larger after time. Many foreigners who have integrated themselves into Bulgarian life, culture and community will be faced with this dietary dilemma. Without being too self-righteous, you would think most foreigners living here would have an advantage, with their knowledge of what is considered a good or bad diet, but do we? Look at where you come from, it there a glut of obesity there?

(Facts and figures taken from The Institute for Marketing and Social Surveys MBMD Research)

SIMPLE TREASURE - 59

- Coriander -

Since I discovered that coriander is grown in Bulgaria I decided to find out a bit more about it. Bulgarians export all their homegrown coriander, and it's a slight mystery as to why they don't use this exciting ingredient in their cooking. It may be that it's too spicy for Bulgarian tastes. Having grown this very successfully in England before coming here, even selling coriander produce to customers on eBay, I believe it is something of a well worth taking on here, with ideal growing conditions. There are many varieties of coriander, all of which can be used, whole, ground and the leaves that have many uses.

Whole coriander seeds are used in pickling and for special drinks, such as mulled wine, whereas ground coriander is often used in baked foods, curry blends and soups. Ground coriander quickly loses its flavour and aroma, so it is best to keep the seeds whole in an air tight container and when a recipe calls for ground coriander, freshly grind whole seeds just prior to use. To heighten the flavour of coriander even more first toast or gently dry fry the whole or ground seeds. It should be used sparingly with delicate ingredients or its flavour will overpower everything else. Coriander leaves are widely used in many countries that employ other spicy ingredients. Ground coriander is a major component of garam masala, a basic spice mixture used in Indian and Pakistani cuisine, and coriander leaf is what gives many fresh salsas and ethnic dishes their bite. The fresh leaves and stalks may be used like parsley, but be careful not to overcook the leaves. Coriander is also a perfect complement to any combination of garlic, cumin, oregano, onions, ginger, and chilli peppers.

When picking or buying, choose leaves with an even green colour and no sign of wilting. Pick coriander along with the roots and put in water and cover with a damp cloth until used — it will keep for up to one week in the fridge like this. Whole seeds keep for a year or more if stored in airtight cool places. A good tip, one I use for parsley, but it works just as well for coriander: Then fresh leaves are available, liquidise them into a pulp with some water, then freeze the mixture in ice cube trays. You will retain all the flavour of the fresh coriander leaves; they can be then be used in cooking all year round. There is no reason why you cannot enjoy coriander moments in Bulgaria throughout the year and introduce your Bulgarian neighbours to the flavour of your homegrown produce.

Directly you plant your coriander you may well find that the local ant population just come along and carry them all off to their nests, so you need to be aware of this and replant areas that have been looted. Many people think that their coriander has not grown, but it's simply because ants have nicked the seeds!

- Bulgarians Make, Don't Buy! -

Things you see, hear and experience here in Bulgaria just go on educating you all the time. This was another instance where spending hard earned cash for something that was needed could quite easily be avoided by recycling. Baba Mama shows me the way to prudence, but there has never been any other way for her. After a hard day at work, I returned to my Yambol home one afternoon and there was our Baba Mama: eighty-three and still a sprightly woman, sitting on her donated office swivel chair. The hard plastic wheels had fractured many years ago from use. Baba was smiling as she saw me come through the squeaky metal garden gate. Sitting there under the warm Yambol sunshine, she had a very grey-coloured crocheted dress on her lap. The dress was old, having seen countless decades of wear. It was a handmade dress, and had come in an out of fashion many times since first being crafted by skilled female hands. I didn't think much of it at the time — I thought she was simply repairing the garment, but I did wonder why this thick, crocheted garment was being repaired now, with many more months of hot weather to come and no need for such clothing! And why was it being taken out now, after never being worn for all those years?

An hour or so later she was still there, tinkering with the dress, and I could see lots of wool thrown around the yard, being collected and stored in the cracks in the concrete by the ants on the ground. Now it looked as though she was taking the dress to pieces, and my curiosity was triggered. She said she was going to make a crocheted tablecloth, as we needed one for the dining room table to protect the tabletop from hot dishes. I still just didn't get it at that point, thinking that she was taking a seam out of the dress to perhaps alter the shape somehow, to form a circular or rectangular tablecloth. It was only after nearly two hours of plucking out the seams that held the garment together, that the process of uncrocheting began, by which I mean that the wool was being unravelled and turned into a ball of wool. It was at this point that I realised this was going to be crocheted again from scratch into the needed tablecloth.

A full four hours of un-weaving the dress had elapsed, and the result was a very large, almost football-sized ball of wool that any giant cat would have loved to play with. Here was tablecloth material ready for crotchet action, and it had taken half a day to get to this stage. The very next day, after work, I sat at the table to find that Baba Mama had started the tablecloth crocheting and it would be some time before the completion of the job, perhaps a couple of weeks or so. As with all Bulgarians, time is the least important factor here. It might take up to a month or more to finish the tablecloth, with countless hours of work involved, but that's how it has always been.

It is a fact that this recycling goes on without even thinking by Bulgarians. Certainly the thought that I needed a tablecloth would instantly produce a plan of a trip to the shops to buy one! But not here; if we need something we'll make it from something else. Even all the plucked-out cotton and wool was collected from the yard and placed in a big metal paint pot, which had been salvaged many years ago, and was full of other easily-ignited material, collected as tinder for the winter wood burner (petchka). Buying firelighters, or for that matter a metal bucket to store fire-lighting material in, has never entered her head in all her eighty-three years.

SIMPLE TREASURE - 61

- Box of Bulgarian Chocolates -

In almost every shop in Yambol you will see displays of chocolates, the biggest being taken up by Nestlé. Now I hate the Nestlé company, for many reasons of principle, but many Bulgarians hate Nestlé for the very simple reason that they are more expensive. The shops make sure that the boxes of chocolates are very well presented to the bypassing shopper, with the Nestlé brand always strategically placed at eye level! It seems that they have an over-riding dominance over the market here, and know how to psychologically drive customers to buy their products. Galia is no exception: I quite often remind her of the reasons why she shouldn't buy Nestlé, and their profit-making tactics usually fail at this point.

Most Bulgarians have a sweet tooth; you can tell by the state of many Bulgarian teeth. In fact the only reason many Bulgarians don't eat sweets and chocolates is due to the fact that their teeth and gums are in an awful state of pain when eating, or they haven't any teeth left to dispose of the harder varieties of sugar- based goodies. The whole point of the towering boxes of chocolates is to sow the seed of a reason for buying them. They look so attractive with their tinselled ambience and the supposed contents replicated on the box cover. (Although you would probably suffer if you ate the original chocolates pictured on the box — their gleaming countenance is surely due to a heavy coat of varnish!)

But however could anyone not have a reason to buy a box? And so it becomes a compromise: we succumb to buying a box — but not Nestlé. The time it takes for us to choose which box of chocolates is quite bizarre. Galia will look, and initially point to a Nestlé product, and I'll remind her of the moral grounds for not buying them. Then she will ask me which we should get. I choose, but without thought, of course, as I'm a man. Galia will then correct me in my decision, as invariably my choice is the wrong one: a foible that appears to be a worldwide phenomenon, not restricted to Bulgarian women.... So the chocolates are bought for whatever reason and are taken home, but they don't last long: as we all know there is always a reason to celebrate something in Bulgaria, whether a birthday, a name day, numerous other religious festivals, a national holiday to commemorate some historical landmark in Bulgarian history; the list goes on. Then there is pig slaughtering day, lamb day in the spring, even a chicken day! On all these days chocolates are used either as gifts or hospitality while receiving guests.

Strangely these chocolate treats are never bought purely for the sake of wanting to eat them: there has to be a reason for them to be offered in Bulgaria. I discovered this one day when I suddenly had a pang for chocolate. As the box was taken from the larder Galia's son Ivo appeared, and I presented the box to him first. His response was, 'What's the occasion?' The answer was a craving for chocolate, but this wasn't deemed to be a celebration in itself, and he refused to take one on that point. Galia explained to me that Bulgarians only offer chocolates for a special occasion. My argument was the fact that we had the box of chocolates in the larder was reason enough for a celebration. With this debate over, and conveyed in my best Bulgarian, we all eventually took a chocolate from the box to celebrate that very principle. After all, it is the Bulgarian way and nature of the people to seek celebrations. This evening, just like every evening, we do our little bout of shopping and yet again we find another box of chocolates within the confines of shopping bag. These will be eaten, but not before talking our way into finding an excuse to do so.

SIMPLE TREASURE - 62

- Gardening in Bulgarian Graves -

I had only a vague memory of the first time when, with Galia and her family, I visited an enormous graveyard a few kilometres south of the outskirts of Yambol. It was a particular Saturday in May when everyone in Bulgaria tends to the family graves and it is an important day, as loved ones are remembered and respected. This year I had a better understanding of the social significance. We had the whole household travelling with us as we made our way to the shops early in the morning. It was shaping up to be a very hot day — the early start was to ensure that the humidity wouldn't affect our Baba Mama too much when tending to the graves. As Baba said, 'We don't want another addition to the graves today!' She does have a good Bulgarian sense of humour, and no subject is taboo.

Before we left, a big bottle of water and a couple of gardening tools were put in the boot of the Lada. As with all occasions we were all dressed in neat but practical clothing, as we knew we were going to get a bit dirty with the work ahead. On arrival at the supermarket, only because it was en route to the cemetery, we discovered a 'fast food' takeaway shack, but this was Bulgarian traditional food served up before your very eyes. We had to wait for the food to be cooked, so while Galia and Ivo went off to do the shopping I was left to watch the maestro chef do his work, with Baba quite content to be left behind in the Lada, its windows rolled down on this beautiful day, listening to traditional Bulgarian music.

They returned with many sweets and snacks but strangely no flowers. I thought the sweets and snacks were for us; as for the 'fast food' for four, well I thought it was going to be a long morning and we would have a picnic in the graveyard! All would become clear later... We were off again, with the breeze coming in the speeding Lada's windows cooling us all down. It was only a short drive before we pulled into the cemetery car park, and it was then that I realised why Galia didn't buy flowers in the supermarket: there before us must have been about thirty different flower sellers, from static stalls to individuals with a bucket. This market wasn't licensed by any means; you could just turn up and sell your flowers to visitors. The car park had individual parking lots allocated with white lines marking them out but typically in Bulgaria, they were hardly used; every driver parked on the other side of the road where the flowers stalls were. This was very practical, as they didn't have to walk the ten metres from their assigned parking spaces. Being English, I of course conformed, and parked neatly between the white lines, only to be blocked in by two cars following me who did it the Bulgarian way! Did I get annoyed? A year or so ago I may well have done, but now only with myself, for not being as practical as the other drivers.

The flowers were in abundance and the choice and variety immense; this made it much harder to choose, and as we wandered up and down the numerous sellers presented their floral treasures. With so much competition between the traders the prices were unbelievably low, much lower than in the supermarket, and the quality far higher, so this was the place to buy. It was refreshing to see these local traders having some success in competing with the supermarkets! Next stop was the candle stall; these were to be lit and used later, as tradition stands firm here. You couldn't get these candles in the supermarket, they are uniquely bought in Bulgarian churches, graveyards stalls and the 1-leva bargain shops scattered around towns in Bulgaria.

We were now all ready to go into the graveyard, but why were see so many cars parked outside? Last year all the cars drove into the graveyard and parked there. It wasn't long before, to our annoyance, we found the reason: just like many other things here, a money-making scheme had been put in place. They were now charging a 1-leva entrance fee for each vehicle to enter. Two years ago it was free to park anywhere in Yambol, now barriers are up and charges levied everywhere. This is what it is happening in Bulgaria now and a sense of injustice was felt by all of us as we paid the fee and drove on. It was too far for Baba to walk, as the graves were at the far end of this enormous park, so we had no choice really.

We found the first grave, parked up next to it and disembarked, taking the water, garden tools, candles and some sweets and snacks. All made sense bar the snacks; what were they for? As we made out way to Galia's first husband's grave, we passed another family out tending to one of their relative's graves. Our snacks were distributed to this family, and they returned with food for us in exchange. So, the snacks were brought as an offering to others, as part of a continuing tradition. What a lovely notion, complete strangers exchanging gifts as part of an ongoing ritual. It was so uplifting to be part of this. All the gravestones are very similar in style: even going back fifty years it hasn't changed at all.

Every stone has a framed portrait of the person laid to rest, along with the usual name and dates. No epitaphs are inscribed. In fact that again was refreshing, to see where every grave was in the main equal in status. There was an occasional sculptured bust of one or two individuals, but generally all the graves are simple and kept to traditional dimensions and stature. Communist ideals still remain for the dead, no doubt, and why not? We are all equal at this point.

The grave was now tended to: weeds cleared, fresh flowers laid, candles lit and put in place and prayers said by each member of the family. I stood to one side and didn't interfere with the rituals that went on. It was just good that this still goes on and that memories and respect remain paramount in Bulgaria. The candles usually had a windproof device, in typical homemade and practical Bulgarian fashion. Big oilcans were placed upside down and one side cut out, making an ideal windproof environment to place candles. The long, thin yellow candles were easily pushed into the earth covering the grave and the oil-can covers placed over them.

We visited three other graves in different locations: Galia's father, uncle and grandparents' graves. Baba mentioned she wanted to be laid to rest with her husband as we tended that particular grave. We had three generations of family here with Baba, Galia and Ivo, the three representatives of each one. It was wonderful to see such a close-knit family, upholding the tradition of this third Saturday of May. It was quite strange, but at no time was there any sombre atmosphere during the whole morning, nor was anyone visibly upset. It was as if they had come to terms with the death a long time ago, and this was more of a celebration in memory of their lives rather than a mourning event.

As we drove out Ivo joked saying that we had to pay one leva to get out of the cemetery. This may be the case next year Baba added, and she laughed and giggled all the way home. We got home and it was all out of the Lada, good clothes off to be washed, a change of outfit and the day's routine went on as though nothing had happened earlier. The 'fast food' bought earlier was laid on the table and we all sat down to eat, accompanied by a few beers.

SIMPLE TREASURE - 63

- Bulgarian Tattoos Forever -

Tattoos are rife in Bulgaria; there are countless Bulgarian friends and acquaintances bearing tattoos, and it's a growing fashion here, especially for the younger generation. For the foreigner, tattoos in these lands are bargains to be had: professional tattoo work of high quality is freely available everywhere at low prices. Last year my brother, who over the years has built up an enormous number of tattoos, decided to try adding to this in Bulgaria. Not only was he over the moon with the price and quality, he wanted to treat Galia and her son Ivo for finding him the tattoo artist and to thank her for the help whilst he was here. Ivo was already christened with a few tattoos, but Galia was at this point tattoo free but was adamant she wanted the gift and took it gratefully. She went through the painful process. It was simple design: inked in black, five separate Chinese characters spelling out the word 'Galia', inscribed vertically down the top of her back. She was very happy with the gift and the tattoo, now standing proudly, will attract attention for years to come.

That was a year ago and the tattoo had become part of Galia's character and that's where I thought it might end. Then Galia recently said she wanted another tattoo, and booked it in to our schedule the following weekend. I had forgotten all about it by the time the weekend arrived. It was a beautiful warm sunny Saturday, no work to do, so we decided to go for a stroll in the town. First stop was the tattoo shop to remind me of what she said earlier in the week. She really was going to get another tattoo then but I should have known — she always does what she says she is going to do. The shop was small but modern, set in a terrace of other small shops just a block away from the mainly pedestrian walkway through Yambol town centre. There were Venetian blinds on the big windows preventing us from looking in; the shop was closed. The times of opening were laid out in easy-to-read Bulgarian and on Saturday it was a 10:00 start. We were fifteen minutes too early, but I knew that this was all Bulgarian time anyway, and the decision to wait there was a bad one. Galia of course was used to waiting and had no qualms about just standing there; I always had to be doing something and it felt like a waste of time just waiting. Galia won the case of course and we settled down to wait.

During this time we were greatly entertained by drivers coming up this narrow side street to try and enter the main walkway into town. Today was not a good day for doing this: a much-respected policeman was waiting at the top of the road; he loved his work, and today his job was telling drivers, with great authority, that they couldn't pass. It was end of term and the local school was holding an open day; with crowds of parents and school children milling around, traffic was basically banned in that area. Kindergarten music was blaring out in the public street, and there was a party atmosphere in the town. The funniest thing about the redirection of traffic was that there weren't any signs or indications that the road was closed. It seemed as if this was deliberate, to give this lone policeman the satisfaction of personally sending cars back down the single-track road. Of course most had to mount the pavement, scraping the bottoms of their cars on the high-rise kerbs. Delivery vans were the most entertaining, as they literally bashed their way back down the street, the smaller vehicles lined up behind them having to get out of their way by whatever means.

Still waiting, we watched another entertaining show of builders a hundred feet up working on the edge of a new apartment complex being built. With no scaffolding or perimeter surround them they were within centimetres of plunging to the several storeys to the street. It made me feel very nervous watching, as they hammered and sawed their way around, dicing with death. Waiting there certainly wasn't boring with this going on all around us.

Ten o'clock was now a distant memory. The shop owner next door knew we had been waiting. He was a long-haired heavy-metal merchant who owned a balloon and party shop, and with the end of the school term there much business to be had. Between the stream of children and parents, he noticed that we had been standing around patiently but getting increasingly frustrated. Being Bulgarian and ever helpful, he rang his business neighbour, and pass on the news that he would be there to open up at 11:00. Still, with a little Bulgarian experience under my belt, I doubted very much whether he would be there at 11:00. We went off to do other things; arriving back at 11:15, the blinds in the big windows were up but there was no tattoo maestro in sight and the shop was still closed. It was now almost midday when the maestro finally arrived and we could get down to the business of Galia's tattoo.

It was a huge surprise, and I was at a complete loss for words, when Galia said she wanted my name tattooed on her forearm! I questioned why on earth would she want to do that? The simple answer came back 'I love you very much!' It was still very hard for me to accept that this was what she was doing, but it went ahead; as I said, Galia normally does exactly what she says she is going to do. The Chinese symbols were looked up on the Internet and printed out. Then a transfer was made from the printout and positioned on her arm. A couple of reprints were made until the positioning right, and the needle prepared. All over the walls in his studio there were certificates of the awards he had received. Apart from the certificates and qualifications in the art, he had won major competitions held in Sofia: best of the show, 2nd best in the show and 3rd place only last year. He was obviously held in high esteem, and it was reassuring that Galia was in safe and talented hands.

A few moments later another customer entered: it was Katia with her son, another friend and daughter, whose birthday party we went to last year. Greetings were and goodbyes exchanged, but not before a catch up on all the news in the middle; the tattoo artist joined in the conversation as he worked. With the tattoo complete, cling film was taped over the freshly ink-injected area; we paid the 40 leva and went to celebrate with a shopska salad and a drink in the warm lusciously-green garden area of a nearby restaurant, where a table for two was put in the shade of a tree next to a fountain. So the tattoo was complete, and still I am lost for words with my name on Galia's arm. Well, Bulgarians certainly don't have any problem about expressing their feelings. And me, I know I'm here with Galia for as long as that tattoo stays.

SIMPLE TREASURE - 64

- Gergyovden -

The 6th May is an eagerly day anticipated by the entire Bulgarian population — this is another name day in Bulgaria, a pretty big one as the name is George. Incidentally it is also Army Day to coincide with this day of celebration. It is unofficially the day summer starts, and is celebrated by farmers throughout the land with specially baked Gergyovden bread. All the people that have a name remotely similar to the name George are included in the name day celebrations, but of course all friends and family get in on the act of celebrating on their behalf. So Galia has her name day set today, a special day for her and I had bought a present the day before. No jewellery or fancy fashion items — she wanted a chip fryer, and I was happy to oblige. What a practical Bulgarian she is and a very happy one, I'm so glad I've got her for so many reasons, not least the love I have for her. We had also purchased the lamb — the traditional food of this particular name day — after surveying many shops, but little did we know that we wouldn't get the chance to eat it, mainly because of a surprise guest who arrived at lunchtime. It was Georgio, Galia's cousin, who of course was celebrating his name day too. He had a friend in the wonderful Yambol Park who owned a restaurant bar, and Georgio had reserved an area sitting out in the park for all his friends and family. We had formally been invited and we had to be there within the hour. No worries though, a Bulgarian hour can last anything up to six hours; in some cases forever… This meant that we had time enough to get ready. We were very excited as we remembered last year's celebration laid on by Doctor Georgio; although we didn't make it due to work commitments, we saw how much fun was had from the pictures, including live accordion music and a game involving a live, loaded handgun — but that's another story.

Galia and I got ready in our best outfits and bought a gift of perfume and chocolates for Georgio; traditional gifts with moderate costs are customary. We walked in glorious sunshine to the park (called Diana Park, after the Greek goddess of hunting). We saw the cluster of buildings in the centre of the park, part of which used to be for wedding functions etc. but had been run down since 1990. We could see Georgio in the distance, already with a few friends around him and the rakia beginning to flow. Would he last the distance? We joined them in the middle of the beautiful park; every so often more friends and family turned up. Shopska salad, green salad and nuts came in a never-ending supply from the restaurant and we could smell the herbed kyufte balls on the barbecue. After a few hours the lamb was served, so tender it fell off the bone.

All this time we were talking to a backdrop of heavy metal music; Georgio and Toma (the restaurant owner) were big fans. The park reverberated to the strains of Iron Maiden, Metallica and Alice Cooper; the latter they played at my request once they found out I was a big fan. This occasion was the first time I felt as though I were part of the family; my Bulgarian was now good enough by this point to hold a conversation, no longer did I have to become isolated because of my lack of communication skills. Oddly enough everyone wanted to speak English to me, but I didn't feel right about this and had to keep explaining why.

The guests were still flooding in and the children playing around the tables. It was refreshing to see kids playing without needing constant supervision from parents. They were content to play simple games in the park such as hide and seek, running races or simply messing around with a stick they found in the woods. There wasn't any need for anything for them to be stimulated by other than playing by themselves. The whole day and evening was stress free and content, and having children around added to this immensely. It reminded me of how glad I was that we're here in Bulgaria; they were a real contrast to many of the disrespectful and untamed kids I had the displeasure of teaching in England.

I spoke with many of the guests, including one who was the head coach of the International Bulgarian basketball team, Ivaylo Stoimenov. He was told me how Bulgarian basketball was on the up, and that the Yambol team was the best in the country. He also said that it was becoming harder each year because of a lack of funding in schools. This of course means less talent cultivated at an early age and less talent in the pipeline for the future. He had been the coach for some twenty years, having worked his way up through the ranks. We spoke about many other things related to sport and basketball in particular: he had strong opinions about golf and snooker, and believes that sports that don't involve aerobic activity aren't sport at all! He has a point.

So many friendly people, it is overwhelming that this now is part and parcel of how life is here and Galia and I are also very much part of the makeup. The feasting, drinking, music and song continued on into the night, as the lights came on. Rakia by the litre and real Russian vodka were the staple drinks: every few minutes a big 'Heidi!' would ring out, followed by a 'Nazdrave!' Occasionally a few Bulgarian songs, based around the name of George could be heard, followed by another 'Nazdrave,' and so it went on. Finally the crowd around the long table dwindled as midnight approached; a great evening of laughter and talking, with a bit of dancing toward the end (the two name day celebrities — Georgio and Galia — gave a good demonstration here). We knew we'd been to a party, as we'd lost count of the number of rakias we'd had. Even so, nobody got out of hand; there were no bad words or bad feelings, all was concord yet high-spirited throughout. Again, the respect everyone has for everyone else here is quite astounding. When we finally got home and looked at each other, we know that coming back home to Bulgaria was the best move we had ever made; we just don't want to ever leave again.

SIMPLE TREASURE - 65

- Monster Banks in Yambol -

Things have changed in Yambol over the last few years. Just three years ago this was quite a sleepy town, with little shops, cafes and tucked-away restaurants galore. The town had so much character thanks to these quirky and individually styled little ventures that Yambol felt unique in this world of cloned businesses. It is now 2008, three years on, and now that we are in the EU, with all the uniformity that comes with it, Yambol has changed. Monsters have appeared in its midst, and are destroying the very fabric that once gave this town its soul. What are these monsters? Well there are many forms of monster invading Yambol: 4x4 vehicles, supermarkets and tourists, but the most prominent, by their very nature and the locations you find them, are the banks. When I first arrived here there were probably three or four banks in the town, with maybe two or three cash points within the confines of a couple of them. What do we find now? Just off the top of my head there must be fifteen banks at least that have forced their way into the town. I have actually lost count of the number of cash points there are so many, and they are not just at the banks. In small shops, garages, malls, everywhere you look you will see cash points popping up like a serious outbreak of measles.

Banks are indeed evil monsters: they rob the poor and give to the rich. Their whole principle is to make money, like any other business, but the way they do it is criminal. In an allegedly fair and democratic society, how can the principle of taking more money from the poor and rewarding the rich be totally accepted? What we actually do is give banks our money, and pay them for that. They get interest from our money and still charge us more on a monthly basis for doing that in Bulgaria. When opening up a new account a couple of months ago I had to pay them money to do so! Paying them money to give them money! I was angry, but the Bulgarians accept all the time that they have to pay for a service. Paying a utility bill has to be done through a bank: it is more expensive doing it this way, as the bank charges a fee for the service. I have not been given any option, and feel quite cheated that this is the only method of payment; no doubt a deal was struck between the Bulgarian utility companies and the greedy banks!

Many people in Bulgaria have to get loans and credit, not mortgages, as they can no longer afford property due to the poor wages in relation to property prices. The loans are for cars, mobile phones and repairs to homes. Typically, those who need loans are the poorer proportion of Yambol folk. They have to pay interest rates that are higher because of the relatively small amounts they have to borrow. Again, this is yet another unfair system in place with the banking systems. At the other end, if you have large assets the bank pays interest for keeping it in the bank. Who pays for this interest? Quite simply the poor as they pay grossly inflated funds from the higher interest on the little loans given to them. So the rise in the number of banks in Yambol is down to bad business ethics, jumping on the bandwagon of extorting the poor.

The other side to banks is that they are sterile buildings with no character or soul. I used to frequent a lovely café on the corner in the town centre, where sitting out and drinking lemon tea, watching people walk past, was a wonderful pastime. Suddenly one evening, only a few weeks later a bank has replaced it! A small white goods store where I used to shop just did a disappearing act, and has been replaced by another bloody bank. Yet another that used to be a great kitchenware shop was knocked up into a post bank over Christmas. There are at least three or four other shops that we used to love browsing round and socialising in that have now passed away, and monstrous banks have engulfed them in each case. How I hate what I see: Yambol is fast becoming a faceless shopping town with the spread of these uniform and characterless bank buildings. What makes it worse is they invariably take up town centre positions, staring you in you face. How long can this go on for? They say that progress speeds up as time goes on. More than ten banks built in the last three years; how many more over the next three years? Bulgaria's economy is still very much cash driven, but unfortunately this will come to an end before we know it. Good news for other Europeans here, but such a shame that Yambol and other towns in the country will lose their identity in the influx of EU and western influences.

SIMPLE TREASURE - 66

- Outside Toilets Preferred -

It's a mystery as to why some here people chose outside toilets in preference to the indoor purpose built system that we now have in civilised parts of the world. The reason I mention this is the countless times I've seen Bulgarians preferring nature as their first choice. The first time I noticed this was in my own Skalitsa farmhouse; the renovated extension has a bathroom with all the modern facilities within, but guests — Bulgarian guests that is — absolutely refuse to use it. They either use my outside toilet in the field or in some cases go round the back to the stable and relieve himself or herself by a wall or the rain drain. This I can understand to a degree, as many guests in the village aren't used to using inside toilets, and a few have never even seen one!

Skalitsa village toilet habits are one thing, but in the town of Yambol you would think that inside toilets would be a common choice for townies. That's what I thought at first, but then it became quite clear from the evidence that this didn't hold. The first instance was Bulgarian women not using the restaurant toilets, but waiting until the walk home then using the side of an apartment block wall while I played lookout. Home, with an inside toilet, is only a couple of metres away, but they prefer the street. This is not a one off instance but done on a regular basis.

Walking in the park, they choose the bushes, even when we had a name-day party in the park the inside toilets weren't used: the women used the bushes and the men used the Tundzha River. Even by the bus garage, where there are public toilets, most people will walk straight by these and use the wall around the back of the toilets. There is a good reason for that though, there is a fee to use the inside toilets! Driving anywhere with guests, they choose to stop and relieve themselves by the side of the road rather than wait until we get to our destination or home, even if the journeys are very short.

In the house we have a lovely inside toilet. We often sit outside in the front yard/garden, and I have lost count of how many times our Bulgarian household use the drain by the wall or the bucket that sits under the outside tap as a toilet. Not only do the house members use this, but other guests and neighbours do exactly the same thing. There is no stigma attached by doing this, no scruples or embarrassment. To the Bulgarians going to the toilet is very much an everyday activity and they will not bat an eyelid seeing someone relieving themselves in public. You see it all the time here, Bulgarian men parking and relieving themselves by the side of the road while a stream of traffic drives past. The Bulgarian women are a bit more discreet, but then I suppose they have to be.

It seems this fashion is built into Bulgarian culture, perhaps to save on water: it does make sense not to waste gallons of water when it's not necessary. From that point of view I find myself occasionally doing the same thing away from inside toilet locations. Holding on painfully just doesn't seem worth it if there are trees or a quiet spot around. What harm is it doing anyway? There is more harm flushing a toilet, that for sure. Bulgarians are so practical.

SIMPLE TREASURE - 67

- Shoppe Style Cheese Recipe -

Shoppe style cheese has its roots in Sofia. I hadn't sampled this delightful vegetarian snack until I met Galia. She took me to a Bulgarian restaurant in Yambol to try this dish out, then asked me to compare with her own cooking. Both were excellent, but Galia's had the edge, not least as it was made in the village of Skalitsa, using all homegrown ingredients from my own farm. The recipe is easy and makes a great main meal.

Ingredients:

500g sheep's cheese (sirene)
40g butter
1-2 tomatoes
1-2 peppers
black pepper
paprika
5 eggs

Method: Cut the cheese into five equal slices and place into butter-lined earthenware bowls. Top with tomato slices, pepper rings and some butter, then bake in a hot oven for 5-6 minutes. Break an egg on top of each bowl, add the remaining butter with some pepper and paprika, then return to the oven and bake until a crust is formed. Serve hot, garnished with slices of tomato, some parsley and a chilli.

SIMPLE TREASURE - 68

- An Evening With Rano -

The bedroom had to be redecorated in Galia's house; it was a big job and had to be done by others, as we just didn't have time with out work commitments and low energy levels. A 'maestro' called Lubo did the work for us. Our neighbour who lived two doors along originally introduced Lubo to us; his name was Rano. We assumed Rano was Lubo's boss, and we found it funny that for the five days Lubo worked in the house, Rano was never seen at any time. Lubo did a good job putting up the plasterboard walls and painting them light orange, but that's all he did, and like any other good Bulgarian worker, didn't finish off jobs. He didn't fit back in any of the sockets and lights switches he'd taken out, the skirting board wasn't replaced and the wall protruded to a degree that the door couldn't open more than 90 degrees without damage. This is normal, and we didn't contest any of this when he said goodbye for the last time.

Rano came around just after Lubo had 'finished' work. It was clear that Rano wasn't entirely sober as he was helped up the steps and led into the bedroom to view the work. This again is normal: it was a Sunday, and late afternoon. After the work had been surveyed and given the thumbs up, Rano discovered that the Englishman living there spoke an understood a little Bulgarian. So he took me to one side and that was the start of a long evening....

Rano told me all about himself: he was 57 years old; his wife had passed away some twelve years ago. He now lived with his daughter and granddaughter, and explained that he had been celebrating earlier as it was his granddaughter's first birthday. Rano is of medium build with jet-black hair, hardly any sign of greyness. I asked him if he dyed his hair; he laughed and said all the rakia kept his hair black, with no sign of baldness.

He was interested in the tomatoes outside in the garden; as he pointed to them he used his middle finger. A little taken aback, I explained that this was a rude way of pointing. I could have curled up and died when he showed me that he had no index finger. He explained that he had lopped it off using a chain saw when he was drunk. To my relief a loud hearty laugh eliminated any embarrassment, and Rano joked that he can only count up to nine and a half.

Rano never stopped talking: he went on to explain that he used to live by the Tundzha river when is wife was alive; they had 12 cows, 40 sheep and a variety of other livestock, and grew produce on the farm. After his wife died he had to sell up and bought a smaller town home. Galia joined in the conversation as Rano changed the topic to rakia, and whether I liked it or not. Naturally I couldn't lie, and that was the rat down the drainpipe; he got up, stumbled off down the flight of four steps and returned five minutes later with a litre of home-brewed rakia as a gift.

I wasn't too sure whether he should have more rakia, as he had had more than a skin full already, but he was a grown man and I supposed he could make that decision for himself. No need to ask whether he wanted more as the ice was brought out from the fridge. From then on there was a constant barrage of 'Nazdrave!' along with discourse on topics far and wide. He wanted to know everything and like all Bulgarians, no subject was taboo. He was also full of self-righteousness as well as rakia; being a

Bulgarian man his views on every topic were from a point of him being right. Rano told us about Mafia-infested Yambol, where not only the big businesses were being suffocated; smaller enterprises were now also being extorted to feed Mafia funds. He saw it every day in his job as a security guard — they stand out like sore thumbs as they come and go in their flash cars and suits.

The subject turned to religion, and I was asked where my beliefs lay. On finding out that I was a protestant he seized the opportunity to call all priests robbers. His finger was out again in that offensive fashion, pointing to God above, saying he was employing these priests who take the money off the good people who go to church. He went on to rail against the fact that there are now shops inside the churches selling second-hand goods to raise more funds for the money-grabbing priests. I have to say he has a point: we live next to a priest who has the most modern and completely renovated house (still being upgraded), with a brand new Mercedes parked outside. This, compared with the other houses and cars in the same street, is proof enough that the priest lives like a king amongst peasants. There of course is a degree of jealousy in the man as his animosity rose during this subject.

We had been sitting at the table for an hour, and in that time he had smoked seven cigarettes. I knew this from the fact that I was putting the butts into a jar of water, making some poison to spray on the flowers in the yard to keep the blackfly and greenfly of them (a trick brought over from England). 'How many cigarettes do you smoke a day?' I asked Rano. It turned out that he got through five packets of 20 a day! He argued that cigarettes were good for your health, and he was a testimony to that fact. He then tried to persuade me to take up the habit, pushing the cigarette packet towards me; he wouldn't give up, but finally settled for me taking one and lighting it up for him. Even then it was a struggle for him to take it back from me!

Rano suddenly laughed out aloud for no apparent reason. We ask what was so funny. He said he had heard that the English keep their dogs in the house. He laughed even harder when I said that many go to bed with them! He just couldn't understand why they would do this. I didn't bother trying to explain, as I didn't really know either.

'How much pension do you have?' was the next question. When I said I didn't have one he suddenly stopped talking and was in deep thought. This man had assumed for some time now that every British subject that comes over here is either loaded or on a big pension. He was totally and utterly shocked. He had never even considered for one moment that I would come over here with nothing and have to work. It took him quite a while to recover from that one, but another rakia helped.

Time ticked on and his tongue clicked on as the subject of pigeons came up. I knew he kept them, as I could see them from the bedroom window, roosting on the roof of his outhouse at the end of the garden. He asked whether I liked pigeons: when I said I love pigeons, but grilled, not fried. When he realised I wasn't joking that sobered him up for a moment. I had already upset my village neighbour, who also keeps pigeons as a hobby by saying they taste nice. Bulgarians love their pigeons, but not for dinner. Another 'Nazdrave!' diffused the situation, and Rano was back to normal. After another sip of rakia, he'd completely forgotten that I like pigeon meat.

The evening went on and on and subject after subject was dissected. The rakia was fast disappearing, mostly going down Rano's throat but twice over the table as his hand fumbled its way to the glass; it was getting more difficult for him to judge the distance between him and his drink. It came to pass when Rano suddenly said he loved me. Even Galia was surprised with that one! It was a term of compliment, of course, but the drink had got the better of him and his dignity was fast disappearing.

It was gone 9:00 and was getting dark as a drunk Rano tried to get us to come home with him for more drink and some food; he offered to start up a barbeque and cook some home-slaughtered lamb as he still kept saying he loved me. We must have said 'No!' at least 50 times but he still insisted on our company; Galia was now getting quite frustrated, and as he turned away every so often we indicated with our hands that he was to go. He was very used to getting his own way, but not with Galia or me that night. We were knackered, having worked all week and all weekend. Gone are the times where I let people tell me what I can and can't do. Besides, the man was beyond reason.

He finally left, after nearly falling down the stairs, but only on the condition we went to his place the next evening for barbeque, salad and rakia. It took a full 20 minutes for him to say goodbye, weaving his way towards his front door. That was Rano: as we went inside Baba said, 'Rano drinks a lot.' My reply? 'I know!'

SIMPLE TREASURE - 69

- Handbags for Bulgarian Men -

The men in Bulgaria have a certain fashion trend at the moment. In summer most guys just wear T-shirts (usually adorned with American motifs, phrases and occasionally swear words) with a pair of shorts and sandals. It doesn't matter where they are: on holiday; working; shopping; eating in a restaurant; that's the normal attire, come what may. The style of T-shirt and shorts depends on where they are. For example, at home they will change into an older T-shirt, paired with shorts and flip-flops. In a restaurant, more formal attire is called for: they will wear their best T-shirt, and leather sandals. This is the Bulgarian way in warm weather. But what caught my eye wasn't this fashion — it was the accessories.

Now, Bulgarian women love their handbags. The men love their handbags too, although it's not called a handbag: it's a shoulder bag — technically, a handbag with a shoulder strap attached. (Incidentally these were first used during WWII). You would be hard pushed to find any Bulgarian man, replete with T-shirt, shorts and sandals, not completing his uniform by donning a shoulder bag. The reasons are quite plain, from the point of view of practicability point.

The pockets on shorts are really quite useless for anything other than perhaps a tissue. If you sit down with anything in your pockets when you stand up and walk off you'll leaving the contents behind. I've lost lots of money doing this, especially getting in an out of cars and sitting on sofas. The Bulgarian man does not want to lose money, that's for sure; not only that, most Bulgarian men carry their Lichna Carta identity document with them at all times. They can't afford to lose that. The other item that is always carried is the mobile phone, or in a lot of cases mobile phones: many Bulgarian own more than one due to the inconsistency of signals from different hosts. Where can they put them?

The shoulder bag is the complete answer to all these problems. I have to concede that I spent two years without one and lost many items in that time. The reason for this was quite simply that I thought it was a bit 'poofy' going around with a handbag on my shoulder. But practicality won out, and over the last year I too have purchased a shoulder bag, and carry all my personal baggage just like other Bulgarian men. I also now have a fine collection of T-shirts and shorts for every occasion, and in town I fit in quite well, another fashion clone walking about.

SIMPLE TREASURE - 70

- Snake Talk -

You see them on the Bulgarian roads; you here stories about them every day in the village; and to be quite honest most Bulgarians absolutely hate them. Snakes. There are snakes in Bulgaria, one or two of which are poisonous. Most of the snakes that are encountered are of the non-venomous variety, but they are frightening, as they can grow to over two metres in length.

Now the reason I'm talking about snakes is that one weekend, on a very warm Saturday night, we had our beloved neighbours Rosa and Sacho to sit with us in the garden. They work so hard it makes you feel guilty about stopping work yourself at around 8:00 in the evening! In summertime the working day starts at 5:30 in the morning and finishes at around 9:00 in the evening. If you know about Bulgarians and what they call work then you know it's not flat-out labouring all that time, but just doing things at work or on the farm, it the duration that takes the toll, not the effort.

Sacho and Rosa agreed to come around at 9:00, but I knew that was not going to happen. So, I started some kyufte (minced hamburgers) on the barbeque at exactly 9:00 and Galia started making the salad at 9:30 both of us knowing that we had another hour before they turned up. The talking eating and drinking commenced for the rest of the evening but the dominating talk was about snakes.

Rosa is absolutely petrified of snakes: no matter how big or small, venomous or non-venomous, she is out of her pram just at the mention of them. Then there's Sacho, who shrugs of the fear by putting his head back and doing the traditional Bulgarian call of 'Aaaaaaayyyyyy!' This can mean a lot of things, but in this case it wasn't a very convincing call, so I know he's not keen on snakes either. I've seen him before when confronted with one: he is a nervous wreck, but his Bulgarian manhood is at stake as he tries to pretend he's fearlessness with them. We often joke about the snakes that Rosa is so scared of, and when the topic comes up, as it does quite often, we ask whether it is big enough for the barbeque and make slicing actions with our hands. Rosa never finds this funny, but we still say it every time, as it still cracks Sacho and myself up.

Today Rosa found a very big snake in her house. Sacho was summoned and arrived on the scene within minutes, but on their return the snake had disappeared. This snake had been in another neighbour's house earlier in the day. This was known as Rosa described the snake as being over two metres in length and slightly bloodstained around the head, she suspected because it had just finished a meal. This was not the case — Sacho has been called to help at the neighbour's house too; they had been just as scared as Rosa, but Sacho plucked up the courage to get a long stick and whack it a few times to stun it, then grabbed hold of its tail and dragged it outside. Then in a lasso fashion he tossed it into the field. Sacho was animatedly miming this whole episode, nearly whacking Rosa as she sat next to him when he got to the lasso part. This thin man, who stood well over six feet high, then stood up and put his hand another half a metre above his head, showing how long this snake was. Just like showing me how big the fish he caught last year was, that had apparently shrunk in his chest freezer when I saw it a few days later. So I knew this snake might be a bit smaller than he made out.

The snake had sought sanctuary in Rosa's house a few hours later to recover — the bloodstains were from the battering Sacho had given it earlier. Right now no one knew where the snake had gone — it was dark and late, and they both had to go back home with the fear of the snake being there. Possibly with vengeance on its mind after the beating it had taken.

The next two hours the talk continued, all stories told about snakes in Skalitsa and the surrounding area. It was claimed that there are no poisonous snakes in Skalitsa, and that they are all found on the slightly higher ground in the nearby village of General Toshevo. I think they just don't want to scare off the Brits in the village. Having said that I've not seen one poisonous snake since moving here; but then I don't go looking for them.

Other stories came out: about the old woman at the bottom of our road who woke up to find seven snakes under her bed one morning; about the snake found in the house opposite mine (Dino's, God rest his soul). This was a massive two-metre snake found in a half-empty sack of potatoes. Dino tied up the sack and put it on his cart, then took it to sell to the gypsies down the road. Well that's Dino for you; he was always open to new ideas for cash-in-hand deals. Rosa admitted that she sees snakes here on a regular basis, maybe once a week, but then she is always on the lookout for them; her house is the last one in the village, and situated next to the local dump, a source of food that attracts many critters. The place is a magnet for scavengers, especially with pigeons on the menu in

Rosa's yard. She will never lose her fear of snakes and to be quite honest she doesn't have much choice other than to live with them.

Our first encounter with a snake was this year when we came back from the UK. Galia was giving the bedroom a spring clean when she found it behind the bedroom door. It was no more that 70 cm long, but that wasn't what I told Sacho as I explained how I got rid of it. A sharp blow to the head with Galia's stiletto shoe was made; this was the only thing that came to hand at the time. The snake darted out into the hallway and disappeared, but after a search we found it snuggled against the vacuum cleaner, whereupon I whacked it again, picked it up and threw it into the yard. I knew it was harmless, but Galia was calling for the death penalty; she loathes snakes as well, and was quite shaken up by the incident.

There were yet more stories about snakes: snakes in cars, snakes in carts, stables and chicken houses; but the favourite place was the outside toilet. The advice was to look before you squat. I was surprised that I hadn't heard many of the stories, but then I have never been bothered by snakes before and don't have a big phobia about them, unlike the rest of the company that night. I really didn't know how they were going to sleep after all the talk about snakes; I get the same sleepless nights talking and thinking about ghosts, so I know how they must feel.

The evening ended with the full moon above us as hungry wolves howled in the distance. This took our minds off the snakes for a while, and briefly onto wolf stories before. Rosa and Sacho pleaded tiredness and went home to — we hoped — a snake-free house. The next morning there was no more on the subject, so the snake is now somewhere else....

- Sarmi Recipe -

Similar to Greek dolmades — stuffed vine leaves — sarmi, like so many other Bulgarian dishes, is completely versatile and totally practical. It can be eaten hot or cold, used as a main course, a side dish or a quick snack. It is much favoured by shepherds who load their lunch bags with sarmi for the long day and summer nights.

Ingredients:

750-800g minced meat (in Bulgaria either pork meat or a mix of pork and turkey meat is used)
1 medium onion, finely chopped
2 garlic cloves, finely chopped
1/2 cup rice
1 cup yoghurt (full fat if possible)
handful of finely chopped fresh parsley
a few sprigs of fresh mint
paprika
about 30-35 large vine leaves
sunflower oil
pepper and salt

Method:

Gently fry the finely chopped onions and garlic in the sunflower oil, adding a little water after a few minutes. Then stir in the paprika and remove the pan from the heat. Add the mince, rice, pepper, mint and parsley and pour some salted water over the mixture before bringing it up to the boil. Turn the heat down and simmer until all the water has been absorbed.

The fresh vine leaves need to be blanched in hot water for 5 minutes. If using preserved vine leaves you just need to rinse them with cold water before using. Lay the vines out flat and put 1 tsp of the mixture in the middle on each vine leaf. Roll the leaf up, tucking in the sides as you go, and place them in a broad-based saucepan. Pour over a couple of cupfuls of warm water and add 1 tsp of oil, then place the lid on and simmer over a low heat for about an hour.

You can serve them traditionally, with the yoghurt and some sunflower oil beaten together, along with a sprinkling of paprika. For a special occasion, place the sarmi on a bed of fresh salad, adding a few slices of orange or lemon to garnish.

Note:
If you have access to fresh vine leaves, pick them in the spring; the surplus can be blanched and preserved in jars of salt water. Bulgarians make sarmi any time of the year by doing this.

SIMPLE TREASURE - 72

- Another Taste of Heaven -

It had been a busy day, and with one thing and another we just didn't have the time to do any shopping. As it turned out I was glad we didn't.... Sitting down that evening, the big question on the women's minds was, what could we give the men to eat tomorrow? Funny as it may sound, this was quite a stress for them. My own answer was to suggest I go to the shopping the next morning and get provisions in — the break and the walk would do me good I argued. That was not an acceptable answer to the solution: it was the women who provided the food, not the men. They just work for the money.

So, the next day no shopping was done, but Baba was messing about in the kitchen as usual. I knew there were potatoes on the menu, from all the peeling the night before, but what else was she doing?

It was midday as Baba waddled over, peering over my laptop screen to whisper 'Haidi munja' — 'Let's go, food!' So it was a curious, and hungry, Englishman who was led into the kitchen where upon the table lays the usual array of gleaming cutlery and side dishes with the main focus on the centre tray. The earlier clue about the potatoes was spot on, but what else was there?

My curiosity was now satisfied: nothing, other than potatoes, bread, garlic and sirene cheese. Not a disappointment by any means, and when tucking into the potatoes I realised how such a simple dish can create such a wonderful experience. Baba instructed me to scatter some sirene on the potato dish and mix it in before eating. So I did just that, and the combination was magnificent. All she had done was boil the potatoes, add some chopped onions, oil and salt; with the addition of the sirene, all the taste buds were having an orgy of enjoyment. And everything in front of me was produced locally in Yambol without a chemical or preservative in sight. A simple meal, but the event of the day: another taste of heaven from the Yambol kitchen table. This is another example of simple treasures in Bulgaria.

Printed in Great Britain
by Amazon